BUILDING HIGH-PERFORMING TEAMS

Strategies for Supervisors

Building High Performance Teams

Strategies for Supervisors

Dr. Patrick C. Patrong

President/CEO
Patrong Enterprises, Inc.

Richmond, VA

Building High Performance Teams: Strategies for Supervisors

For information regarding permissions or speaking engagements, contact:
Patrong Enterprises, Inc.

Richmond, Virginia

Telephone/WhatsApp: 1.410.294.5431

Website: www.patrong.com

Email: info@patrong.com

All examples, case studies, and scenarios in this book are inspired by real organizational settings but are presented in a composite form to preserve confidentiality and learning value. Names, roles, and details have been altered to protect confidentiality.

Printed in the United States of America.

ISBN: 979-8-9998411-3-1

Library of Congress Control Number: *Pending*

Design and Layout: Patrong Enterprises, Inc. **Cover Design:** "PEI Creative Studio 1A

First Edition: 2025

Legal Disclaimer
This publication is intended to provide general leadership and supervisory guidance. It is not intended to substitute for legal, human resources, or compliance advice tailored to any specific organization. Readers should consult their agency or legal counsel before applying any policies or procedures discussed in this book.

.

DEDICATION

To the public servants — the supervisors, managers, and frontline employees — who show up every day with commitment and resolve. This book is dedicated to those who carry the weight of accountability, often unseen but always essential, ensuring that our communities function, thrive, and endure.

To the leaders who believe in fairness, integrity, and opportunity — may these pages affirm your work and encourage you to continue shaping teams that reflect the very best of public service.

Furthermore, to the citizens we serve — may every lesson and every principle shared here remind us that government work is not only about policies and procedures, but about people, trust, and legacy.

TABLE OF CONTENTS

1 UNDERSTANDING TEAMS IN THE PUBLIC SECTOR

Introduction

Teams are the lifeblood of public service. Every street repaired, every permit approved, every emergency response coordinated depends on the effective functioning of teams. Unlike the private sector, where efficiency and profit margins dominate the conversation, government teams operate under the dual weight of accountability and transparency. They answer not just to managers but to citizens, taxpayers, elected officials, and oversight bodies. That is why the role of the supervisor in public sector teams is significant: you are not simply ensuring that the work gets done; you are upholding the very credibility of government service.

In this chapter, we explore what makes public-sector teams unique, why understanding team dynamics is crucial, and how supervisors can apply proven frameworks to lead effectively. We will draw lessons from established theories, such as Bruce Tuckman's model of group development, and also examine the nuances that distinguish municipal and state teams from corporate ones. We will highlight the informal dynamics that often determine success or failure and uncover barriers that commonly derail progress. Through case examples, reflective exercises, and practical checklists, you will gain tools to not only understand your team but also to shape its growth into a high-performing unit.

Section 1: What Makes Government Teams Unique

Government teams are fundamentally different from their private-sector counterparts. While private organizations are judged by their financial performance, public agencies are evaluated by service outcomes, equity, and trust. Supervisors in the public sector operate in a landscape shaped by policy mandates, legislative oversight, budgetary constraints, and heightened visibility. This makes the work of leading a team in government both uniquely challenging and uniquely impactful.

The **first distinguishing feature** of government teams is the principle of **public accountability**. Every action, decision, and outcome can potentially be subject to scrutiny by citizens, elected officials, auditors, or the media. Unlike private companies, where mistakes may be quietly corrected, public-sector missteps can quickly escalate into public controversies. For example, when a city's snow removal team fails to clear roads in time for the morning commute, frustrated residents often turn to social media, local news, or council members for answers. The supervisor leading that team is suddenly thrust into the spotlight, even if the team is working around the clock under severe constraints. This reality makes it essential for supervisors to cultivate transparency within their teams, prepare employees for public interaction, and model composure under pressure.

The **second distinguishing feature** is the **bureaucratic framework** in which government teams operate. Rules and procedures are designed to ensure fairness, equity, and legal compliance, but they can also slow progress. Hiring a new employee may require multiple approvals and a lengthy civil service process. Implementing a new technology may require compliance reviews, procurement protocols, and even council approval. For supervisors, this means that innovation requires persistence and patience. A good idea is not enough; it must be shepherded through established procedures without cutting corners. Supervisors who thrive in this environment are those who teach their teams to balance creativity with compliance — ensuring that staff understand why rules exist while still seeking smarter, more efficient ways of working within them.

A **third feature** of government teams is the **reality of limited resources**. While private organizations can sometimes generate new revenue or reallocate funds quickly, public agencies operate under budgets set by elected officials. These budgets are often fixed, and sometimes reduced, even as service demands grow. Supervisors must therefore learn to do more with less. A parks and recreation supervisor, for instance, may face budget cuts that reduce the number of program staff, yet still be expected to deliver youth programming and maintain facilities. In such situations, the supervisor's role is to foster innovation, encourage cross-training, and make informed decisions about where to focus limited resources. Supervisors who can engage employees in problem-solving, rather than simply relaying constraints, build resilience and morale even in lean times.

Another critical factor is **workforce diversity — not just in demographics, but in tenure, motivation, and employment structure**. Public-sector teams often comprise employees who have worked for decades alongside those who are just entering the workforce. Some staff may be unionized, while others serve in temporary or part-time roles. Supervisors must manage these differences with fairness and consistency. A veteran employee may resist a new system by citing "the way we have always done it," while a younger employee may push for innovation aggressively. Balancing these perspectives requires diplomacy. The wise supervisor leverages the institutional knowledge of long-serving staff while creating space for new voices to contribute. Doing so requires intentional relationship-building and a recognition that diversity, when harnessed well, is a source of strength rather than friction.

Finally, public-sector teams operate under **constant community visibility**. A city utility worker fixing a water line, a state DMV employee processing licenses, or a county health worker administering vaccines — each is a direct representative of government to the public. Unlike back-office corporate employees who may never interact with customers, many public employees are on the front lines every day. Their professionalism, courtesy, and effectiveness directly shape citizen trust in government. Supervisors must recognize this dynamic and coach employees not only on technical competence but also on customer service, civility, and communication. Every citizen interaction is an opportunity to build or erode trust in the institution as a whole.

Public-sector teams operate in a context defined by public trust and confidence. Their mission is service, not profit, and their customers are citizens, not shareholders. This distinction creates several unique challenges:

1. **Transparency and Accountability** – Every decision, meeting, and action can be subject to public record requests, media scrutiny, or legislative oversight. Supervisors must prepare teams for the reality that their work may be scrutinized far more closely than that of private companies.

2. **Bureaucracy and Policy Constraints** – Municipal and state teams must operate within regulations, statutes, and administrative procedures. Supervisors may find their decision-making slowed by multiple approval layers, procurement rules, or union agreements.

3. **Limited Resources** – Public budgets are often constrained, requiring supervisors to achieve more with limited resources. Unlike private businesses that can reallocate funds or expand revenue streams, public teams often must deliver results under fixed or shrinking budgets.

4. **Diverse Workforce Composition** – Public agencies typically employ a diverse range of staff, including long-tenured employees with decades of institutional knowledge, early-career professionals, and individuals working under collective bargaining agreements. Supervisors must balance different motivations, expectations, and work styles.

Supervisor's Tip

In public service, it is better to be consistent than flashy. Citizens may forgive a slow process, but they will not forgive unfairness or favoritism.

Quick Checklist: Key Differences in Government Teams

- Accountability extends beyond the organization to citizens and elected officials.

- Bureaucratic frameworks ensure fairness but can slow decision-making.

- Resources are often limited, requiring supervisors to prioritize and innovate.

- Workforce diversity spans generations, union agreements, and employment structures.

- Community visibility means employees are representatives of the government in every interaction.

These unique conditions make supervising government teams both demanding and deeply rewarding. For every barrier, there is an opportunity: to model transparency, to build resilience under constraints, to harness diversity for innovation, and to strengthen the public's trust in government. Supervisors who embrace these challenges not only lead effective teams but also contribute to a stronger, more credible public sector.

Section 2: Stages of Team Development

Supervisors in government can benefit significantly from understanding **Tuckman's five stages of team development**: Forming, Storming, Norming, Performing, and Adjourning. Nevertheless, in the public sector, these stages often play out differently.

- **Forming**: New teams come together around a project, often driven by a policy shift, a grant requirement, or an emergency response. In this stage, employees look to the supervisor for clarity and reassurance.

- **Storming**: Conflicts emerge over priorities, workload distribution, or interpretation of regulations. In a government office, this may involve debates about compliance, resource allocation, or union concerns. Supervisors must navigate these disputes with transparency and fairness.

- **Norming**: The team begins to align around shared goals. In a city planning department, this might mean adopting standardized procedures for reviewing permits. Supervisors reinforce positive behaviors and ensure team values are consistently applied.

- **Performing**: The team achieves high-functioning collaboration. At this stage, teams within a public health department can coordinate inspections, outreach, and reporting seamlessly, even under external pressure.

- **Adjourning**: Teams disband after completing a project or responding to a crisis. Supervisors should recognize contributions and capture lessons learned to prevent institutional knowledge from being lost.

Quick Checklist: Helping Your Team Advance Stages

- Clarify goals and roles early. sure
- Anticipate and address conflict quickly.
- Reinforce norms and values in daily interactions.
- Celebrate milestones as the team performs.
- Document lessons learned before the team adjourns.

Section 3: Dynamics That Shape Team Performance

Beyond formal structures, public-sector teams are deeply influenced by informal dynamics:

- **Informal Leaders**: In many city or state offices, a senior employee who has "seen it all" may hold significant sway over morale, even if they are not a supervisor. Ignoring these informal leaders risks undermining authority. Engaging them can transform them into allies.

- **Silos and Interdepartmental Tension**: Departments often work in isolation. A city's transportation team might clash with public works over road projects. Supervisors must actively encourage collaboration across silos.

- **Generational Differences**: Although we will not delve into this topic in depth, government teams often comprise employees spanning three or four generations. Supervisors need to recognize differences in communication styles and work expectations without resorting to stereotypes.

- **Public Pressure**: Unlike private firms, government employees often interact directly with frustrated citizens. A DMV clerk or city permit specialist may face daily complaints. Supervisors must buffer teams from undue stress while reinforcing standards.

Did You Know?

Studies show that in public agencies, **trust in supervisors** is the single most significant predictor of employee engagement—more than salary, benefits, or even job security.

Section 4: Common Barriers in Public Teams

Government supervisors often face barriers that can derail otherwise capable teams:

1. **Budget Limitations** – Reduced funding can mean outdated equipment, understaffing, and inadequate training. Supervisors must encourage innovation within constraints.

2. **Resistance to Change** – Long-tenured employees may be skeptical of new technology or policy shifts. Supervisors need to strike a balance between respecting institutional memory and the necessity of adaptation.

3. **External Influence** – Political leaders may change priorities suddenly, leaving teams feeling whiplashed. Supervisors must steady the ship, keeping staff focused on the core mission.

4. **Recognition Gaps** – Unlike the private sector, the government often lacks structured reward systems. Supervisors must find creative ways to recognize contributions—sometimes as simple as a handwritten thank-you note or public acknowledgment at a staff meeting.

Reflection Box

- What barriers does your team face most often?

- How do you currently address them?

- What is one new strategy you can implement this month to reduce these barriers?

Case Snapshot: City Utility Department

A mid-sized city experienced a major water outage due to a burst main. The utility department was overwhelmed with citizen complaints and media inquiries. The supervisor quickly recognized that the team had entered the Storming stage—frustration was spilling into open conflict.

Instead of reacting defensively, the supervisor convened a 20-minute huddle. He acknowledged the pressure, restated the mission ("get safe water back to residents as fast as possible"), and reassigned tasks clearly: field crews to repairs, office staff to communication, and supervisors to updates. He also empowered staff to share real-time information with citizens rather than waiting for approvals.

The shift was immediate. Employees felt supported and had a clear understanding of their roles. Citizens began receiving accurate updates within the hour, reducing anger. Within 24 hours, repairs were complete, and the city publicly praised the utility staff. The supervisor later used this experience as a case study in resilience, helping the team recognize that conflict can be the soil from which collaboration grows.

Practice Exercise

1. Draw a **Team Dynamics Map** of your current team. Place each member along Tuckman's stages: Forming, Storming, Norming, Performing, or Adjourning.

2. Identify two strengths and two challenges your team faces at this stage.

3. Write one concrete action you will take in the next two weeks to move your team closer to high performance.

Summary and Key Takeaways

- Public-sector teams are unique due to their accountability, bureaucracy, limited resources, and the need for public trust.

- Supervisors must understand and navigate the five stages of team development, adapting strategies for government environments.

- Informal dynamics often matter as much as formal structures—recognize and engage with them.

- Common barriers include budget limitations, resistance to change, external pressures, and lack of recognition.

- Supervisors who can identify their team's stage, address barriers, and reinforce purpose can transform ordinary groups into high-performing teams.

"In government work, your team is more than a group of employees—it is the face of public service. Lead them well, and you lead the community itself."

2 BUILDING A STRONG FOUNDATION FOR TEAMWORK

Introduction

Strong teams do not emerge by accident. They are carefully shaped through intentional leadership. In government settings, where employees often serve under civil service protections, union agreements, or tight budgetary oversight, the supervisor plays a critical role in laying the foundation upon which performance, morale, and trust are built. Without this foundation, even the most talented individuals may drift, duplicate work, or lose sight of their shared mission. With it, teams thrive despite external pressures.

The foundation of effective teamwork rests on three interlocking pillars: **vision, roles, and culture**. A compelling vision provides direction, clarity, and inspiration. Clear roles ensure that employees understand expectations, boundaries, and responsibilities. A healthy culture sustains trust, fairness, and collaboration across the team.

Supervisors who invest early in building this foundation reap long-term rewards. Their teams navigate change with resilience, handle conflicts with maturity, and deliver consistent service to citizens. This chapter explores how to establish vision and goals, define roles and responsibilities, and create a culture where employees feel valued and motivated. Each section provides practical strategies, examples from public agencies, and exercises you can apply directly with your team.

Section 1: Establishing Vision and Goals

Vision is the anchor of teamwork. It connects day-to-day tasks to a larger purpose that employees can see and believe in. Without vision, government work risks becoming mechanical and uninspired. Employees may focus narrowly on their assigned tasks—such as processing forms, repairing roads, or answering citizen calls—without understanding how those tasks contribute to the broader mission of serving the community.

Why Vision Matters

A compelling vision does more than inspire; it clarifies priorities amidst complexity. In a city planning office, for example, employees might process dozens of permits each week. Without vision, the work feels transactional. With vision—"Shaping safe, sustainable neighborhoods for all residents"—each permit is reframed as part of a larger purpose. This shift energizes employees, strengthens accountability, and aligns daily efforts with community outcomes.

Supervisors must translate broad agency missions into **concrete team-level goals**. A state department of transportation might declare a mission of "safe, efficient mobility for all citizens." For a highway maintenance crew, the supervisor translates that mission into measurable goals: "Repair all reported potholes within five business days" or "Ensure snow removal routes are cleared within 12 hours of a storm." These goals provide clarity while connecting frontline tasks to the agency's broader mission.

Characteristics of Effective Team Goals

- **Specific and measurable** – Goals should be clear enough that progress can be tracked (e.g., "respond to all citizen inquiries within 48 hours").

- **Aligned with agency mission** – Goals must connect to larger public outcomes, not just internal efficiency.

- **Achievable with available resources** – Unrealistic goals undermine morale, especially in resource-limited government settings.

- **Time-bound** – Goals framed within deadlines create accountability.

Supervisor's Tip

Do not assume employees see the connection between their work and the agency's mission. Spell it out. Reinforce it regularly. Overcommunication is better than silence.

Quick Checklist: Establishing Vision and Goals

- Have I communicated a clear, inspiring vision for the team?
- Do my employees understand how their daily work connects to agency outcomes?
- Are our goals specific, measurable, achievable, aligned, and time-bound?
- Do I revisit goals in meetings, evaluations, and recognition moments?

Reflection Box

- What is the current vision of my team?
- Does it inspire employees, or does it feel like just words on a poster?
- How can I translate the agency's mission into specific goals my team can achieve this year?

When supervisors embed vision into everyday conversations, employees begin to internalize it. Over time, the vision becomes an integral part of the team's identity, shaping how members prioritize their work and evaluate success.

Section 2: Defining Roles and Responsibilities

If vision answers the question "why," then roles answer the question "who does what." In public agencies, where responsibilities can be blurred by bureaucracy or outdated job descriptions, clear role definitions are essential. Without it, confusion reigns, duplication of effort drains energy, and conflict emerges over perceived inequities.

The Dangers of Role Ambiguity

Ambiguity often manifests in subtle ways: two employees assume the other will complete a task, deadlines slip because no one takes ownership, or conflicts erupt when one person feels another is encroaching on "their" work. For example, in a city housing department, if it is unclear whether inspections are the responsibility of frontline staff or senior inspectors, complaints accumulate while employees debate their responsibilities.

Role ambiguity not only reduces efficiency but also erodes trust. Employees want to know where they fit, what is expected of them, and how they will be held accountable. When those boundaries are unclear, morale suffers.

Clarifying Roles in Government Settings

Supervisors in municipalities, cities, and state agencies often inherit teams with outdated or overly generic job descriptions. Updating them formally may take time, but supervisors can still create clarity by:

- Writing role summaries that define each person's core duties.

- Outlining expectations during team meetings.

- Documenting "who handles what" for recurring tasks or projects.

- Revisiting roles whenever the team changes, such as turnover, a new initiative, or a crisis.

Example: In a county emergency management team, the supervisor clarifies:

- One employee is responsible for coordinating communication with the media.

- Another employee handles logistics for shelters.

- A third oversees volunteer coordination.
  By putting these responsibilities in writing and revisiting them

during briefings, the supervisor ensures smoother responses during disasters.

Supervisor's Tip

Role clarity is not about micromanagement; it is about empowerment. Employees perform best when they know exactly where their responsibilities begin and end.

Quick Checklist: Defining Roles and Responsibilities

- Are all core duties documented and shared with the team?
- Do employees know who is accountable for each recurring task?
- Have I clarified expectations when new projects arise?
- Do I revisit role assignments when team composition changes?

Reflection Box

- Where are the most significant gaps or overlaps in my team's roles?
- What is one step I can take this week to create more clarity?
- How will clearer roles help us serve citizens more effectively?

Clear roles also support fairness. In public agencies, where employees are often quick to notice inequities, role clarity reduces perceptions of favoritism. When everyone understands who is responsible for what, accountability increases, collaboration improves, and the team is better positioned to deliver results to the public.

Section 3: Creating a Positive Team Culture

Culture is the invisible glue that holds a team together. In public-sector organizations, where employees often serve for decades and are deeply connected to the community's identity and culture, culture can either be a powerful motivator or a silent drag on performance. Unlike vision and roles, which can be written down and formalized, culture is lived every day through behaviors, rituals, and unspoken norms.

Why Culture Matters

A positive culture fosters fairness, accountability, and a sense of pride in public service. A negative culture breeds cynicism, apathy, and resistance to change. For example, a city clerk's office where employees habitually complain about citizens behind the counter will quickly develop a hostile culture, leading to poor customer service and low morale. In contrast, a supervisor who consistently models respect, acknowledges effort, and celebrates small wins creates a culture where employees treat one another—and the public—with dignity.

How Supervisors Shape Culture

Supervisors are culture carriers. Employees observe how leaders manage stress, respond to mistakes, and treat others. Key cultural levers include:

- **Consistency**: Employees notice whether supervisors apply rules fairly and respond consistently across situations.

- **Recognition**: Culture improves when employees know their efforts are seen and valued.

- **Communication**: Tone and language in meetings, emails, and casual interactions reinforce expectations.

- **Accountability**: Allowing incivility or poor performance to go unchecked sends a cultural message that mediocrity is acceptable.

Did You Know?

Studies of government workplaces reveal that employees who feel respected by their supervisors are **five times more likely** to report high levels of job satisfaction, regardless of salary or opportunities for promotion.

Supervisor's Tip

Policies do not set culture; daily interactions do. Every meeting, every correction, and every word of recognition sends a cultural signal.

Quick Checklist: Creating a Positive Team Culture

- Do I model respect and professionalism even under pressure?

- Am I consistent in applying rules and standards?

- Do I actively recognize effort, not just outcomes?

- Have I addressed incivility or negativity promptly?

Reflection Box

- How would my employees describe our team culture today?

- What small actions can I take this week to strengthen positivity?

- What behaviors am I tolerating that undermine the culture I want to build?

Case Snapshot: Parks and Recreation Department

A mid-sized city's parks and recreation department had been struggling for years. Budget cuts forced the cancellation of popular programs, leaving staff demoralized and citizens frustrated. Employees felt their work no longer mattered. Complaints mounted, and turnover among younger staff was high.

When a new supervisor took over, she began by redefining the team's vision: *"Our mission is to create welcoming community spaces for all residents, regardless of program size."* This reframing shifted the focus from what the department had lost to what it could still provide.

She then worked on clarifying roles. Maintenance staff were told their contribution—keeping parks clean and safe—was foundational to community pride. Program staff were encouraged to focus on community engagement, even with fewer resources. Administrative staff were tasked with ensuring accessibility and equity in scheduling.

Finally, the supervisor concentrated on culture. She introduced "park pride days," where employees and volunteers came together to celebrate small wins such as repairing a playground or launching a free outdoor movie night. She made recognition routine, thanking staff in public meetings and sharing positive citizen feedback.

Within a year, the department experienced a cultural turnaround. Employee surveys reported higher morale, turnover dropped, and citizens began complimenting staff for their friendliness and dedication.

By focusing on vision, roles, and culture, the supervisor rebuilt the foundation of teamwork despite external challenges.

Practice Exercise

1. Draft a one-sentence **vision statement** for your team.

2. List each employee on your team and summarize their **primary responsibility** in one sentence.

3. Share the draft vision and role summary with your team, inviting them to provide input and feedback.

4. Revise based on the discussion until a consensus is achieved.

5. Identify one ritual, tradition, or practice you can introduce in the next 30 days to strengthen culture (e.g., recognition moments, shared reflection time, cross-department coffee chats).

Reflection Questions

- How often do I communicate the team's vision to employees?

- Do team members clearly understand individual responsibilities?

- What aspects of our culture strengthen performance?

- What aspects undermine it, and how can I address them?

Summary and Key Takeaways

- Strong teams are built on a foundation of clear vision, well-defined roles, and a cohesive culture.

- Vision connects daily tasks to a broader mission and inspires a sense of commitment.

- Role clarity reduces conflict, increases accountability, and empowers employees.

- Positive culture is shaped by supervisor behavior, fairness, recognition, and accountability.

- Supervisors who intentionally establish this foundation prepare their teams to handle resource limits, political changes, and public scrutiny with resilience.

"Foundations built on clarity and purpose give teams the strength to *weather challenges and the courage to innovate.*"

3 EFFECTIVE COMMUNICATION WITHIN TEAMS

Introduction

Communication is the bloodstream of teamwork. It carries ideas, decisions, feedback, and trust throughout a team. In public-sector organizations, where supervisors manage employees under constant scrutiny and community visibility, communication is more than a soft skill—it is a matter of public credibility and reputation. A well-crafted email, a respectful exchange with a citizen, or a timely staff meeting can build confidence in government services. Conversely, poor communication erodes trust, slows processes, and creates frustration both inside and outside the agency.

Supervisors often underestimate their role as leaders of communication. They may view themselves as messengers of policy rather than shapers of dialogue. However, communication is not neutral; it shapes how employees perceive their responsibilities, respond to challenges, and perceive fairness. When supervisors invest in effective communication, they establish the tone for collaboration, problem-solving, and delivering high-quality service.

This chapter examines how supervisors can refine their

communication skills, foster openness among employees, and overcome the barriers that frequently impede government teams. You will gain strategies for building credibility through listening, clarity, and consistency, along with tools to encourage dialogue in environments where mistrust or bureaucracy may inhibit openness.

Section 1: Enhancing Communication Skills for Supervisors

Supervisors are the primary link between employees and the organization as a whole. They translate directives from senior leaders into daily instructions, while also communicating employee concerns upward to their superiors. Effective communication begins with the supervisor's own habits.

1. Clarity and Brevity

Government employees often juggle multiple tasks under pressure. Ambiguous or overly complex instructions increase the likelihood of errors. A supervisor who says, *"Handle those files as soon as you can,"* leaves room for confusion. A better approach: *"Please process the permit applications in the red folder by Friday at 3:00 p.m. so we can meet the council's reporting deadline."* Clear communication reduces stress and improves accountability.

2. Listening as Leadership

Listening is not passive. It is an active demonstration of respect. Supervisors who listen well uncover concerns before they become crises. In a municipal finance office, for example, a staff member might mention casually that a new software system feels confusing. A supervisor who listens and probes further may prevent widespread errors in the future.

3. Tone and Body Language

Nonverbal cues often carry more weight than words. A supervisor who rolls their eyes during a staff member's comment signals dismissal, even if their words sound supportive. Similarly, a calm and respectful tone during a heated discussion can de-escalate tension.

4. Feedback that Motivates

Feedback should be specific, timely, and balanced. Instead of saying, "You need to improve your reports," a supervisor might say, "Your last report was thorough, but the data tables were difficult to read. Next time, let us use the standard template so it is clearer for council review.' This approach acknowledges strengths while guiding improvement.

5. Transparency and Honesty

In the public sector, where employees are acutely aware of budgetary and political pressures, honesty matters. If resources are limited or priorities have shifted due to leadership changes, supervisors should communicate openly rather than shielding employees from the truth. Transparency builds credibility, even when the news is difficult.

Supervisor's Tip

If you do not fill in the information, rumors will. Share what you know, acknowledge what you do not, and commit to updating your team as soon as possible.

Quick Checklist: Enhancing Supervisor Communication

- Are my instructions specific and time-bound?
- Do I listen actively and follow up on employee concerns?
- Does my body language match my words?
- Do I provide feedback that is both affirming and constructive?
- Am I transparent about challenges and changes?

Reflection Box

- How do my employees describe my communication style?
- Do they feel heard when they raise issues?
- What one habit could I change now to improve clarity or trust?
- Am I as intentional in listening as I am in speaking?

Section 2: Promoting Open and Honest Communication Among

Team Members

While supervisor-to-employee communication is crucial, high-performing teams also depend on open dialogue among members. In government offices, this can be challenging. Hierarchies, fear of criticism, and union dynamics sometimes discourage employees from speaking openly. Supervisors must create an environment where communication flows freely across the team, not just within the supervisor's sphere of influence.

Building Psychological Safety

Teams thrive when members feel safe to express ideas without fear of ridicule or retaliation. A planning department analyst who hesitates to raise concerns about a zoning proposal may withhold valuable insights that could prevent a costly mistake. Supervisors can build safety by encouraging input, acknowledging contributions, and separating ideas from the people who share them.

Modeling Openness

Supervisors set the tone. If you solicit input but dismiss it, employees will quickly stop sharing their thoughts. Modeling openness means admitting when you do not have all the answers, thanking employees for their candor, and following up when someone offers feedback. Even if an idea cannot be implemented, acknowledging the suggestion respectfully encourages continued dialogue.

Structured Communication Channels

Government teams often rely heavily on email, which can become overwhelming and impersonal. Supervisors can diversify communication:

- Regular team huddles for quick updates.
- One-on-one check-ins for personal feedback.
- Suggestion boxes (digital or physical) for anonymous input.
- Cross-departmental meetings to reduce silos.

Encouraging Peer-to-Peer Dialogue

Supervisors can also foster horizontal communication by assigning collaborative projects or rotating leadership roles among team members. For example, in a public health inspection team, rotating who leads the weekly debrief builds confidence and distributes ownership more evenly.

Did You Know?

Research on workplace collaboration shows that teams with high levels of peer-to-peer communication are **25% more efficient** in completing projects than those that rely solely on top-down communication.

Supervisor's Tip

Encourage the phrase, *"Help me understand your perspective."* It invites dialogue, reduces defensiveness, and shifts focus from debate to discovery.

Quick Checklist: Promoting Open Team Communication

- Do team members feel safe sharing concerns or dissenting views?
- Do I model openness by admitting mistakes and thanking employees for input?
- Have I created multiple channels for communication beyond email?
- Do I encourage peer-to-peer collaboration, not just supervisor-to-employee exchanges?

Reflection Box

- When was the last time a team member disagreed with me openly?
- How did I respond, and what message did that send?
- What structures can I establish to foster more open and honest dialogue?

Section 3: Overcoming Communication Barriers and Conflicts

Even the most committed teams encounter obstacles to effective communication. In government organizations, these barriers are magnified by bureaucracy, resource constraints, and heightened public scrutiny. Supervisors must be skilled at recognizing these barriers and applying strategies to overcome them.

1. Bureaucratic Barriers

Formal processes, approval chains, and reliance on written memos can slow communication. A state agency employee may wait weeks for a response because messages must move through multiple supervisors. To counter this, supervisors can simplify within their sphere of control by holding short team check-ins, setting clear response expectations for internal emails, and utilizing collaborative platforms for routine updates.

2. Hierarchical Culture

Government agencies often have rigid hierarchies that discourage upward communication. Frontline employees may feel that their voices do not matter. Supervisors can break this pattern by creating intentional forums for feedback—such as roundtables, open-door hours, or "pulse surveys"—and by acting visibly on employee input.

Information Silos

Departments may guard information, either due to habit or fear of criticism. This concept leads to duplication of effort and inconsistent service. Supervisors should champion information-sharing by modeling transparency, inviting other departments to joint meetings, and emphasizing the public's need for seamless service.

4. Conflict and Misinterpretation

Conflicts often arise not from malice but from misunderstandings. A facilities crew might feel disrespected if administrative staff overlook the time needed for repairs. Supervisors must address conflicts directly by facilitating conversations, clarifying expectations, and reminding employees to separate the issue from the person.

5. Technology Gaps

Outdated systems can frustrate employees and obstruct communication. While supervisors may not directly control IT budgets, they can train employees to use existing tools effectively and advocate for improvements, providing clear evidence of inefficiency.

Supervisor's Tip

When communication breaks down, do not just look at *what* was said; consider what was not said. Ask *why* the message was not received as intended. The cause often lies in the system, not the people.

Quick Checklist: Overcoming Barriers

- Do I hold regular check-ins to reduce delays?
- Have I created safe spaces for upward communication?
- Am I breaking down silos by sharing information openly?
- Do I address conflict quickly and constructively?
- Am I helping employees use available technology effectively?

Reflection Box

- What barrier affects my team the most today?
- What strategy can I use this week to reduce its impact?
- How will I know communication has improved?

Case Snapshot: Public Health Department During a Crisis

During a flu outbreak, a state public health department struggled with internal communication. Field inspectors were frustrated that they received policy updates days late, after citizens had already asked questions. Central office staff felt overwhelmed by the volume of information and hesitant to release guidance before leadership approval. The result was confusion in the field and rising public frustration.

The supervisor overseeing regional operations intervened. She instituted daily 15-minute conference calls, ensuring that field staff heard updates directly rather than waiting for memos. She also created a simple online dashboard where key updates were posted in real time. Finally, she coached central staff to share draft guidance with clear disclaimers rather than waiting for perfect approvals.

The impact was immediate. Inspectors felt empowered to answer citizen questions, central staff reduced their backlog, and the public received timely and consistent information. The supervisor later reflected that the most important change was not technology, but rather a mindset shift: moving from "wait until everything is perfect" to "share what we know now and update as needed."

Practice Exercise

1. Conduct a **communication audit** with your team:

   o Ask employees what information they need but are not receiving.

   o Identify where delays or misinterpretations occur most often.

   o Map how messages currently flow and where they break down.

2. Choose one barrier and commit to a **30-day improvement plan**. Examples:

   o Introduce a weekly team huddle to reduce email overload.

   o Create a shared folder for common resources.

   o Establish a rule that emails must receive a response within two business days.

3. Reassess after 30 days. Celebrate progress and adjust strategies.

Reflection Questions

- How do communication barriers affect our ability to serve citizens?

- Do I encourage upward feedback, or do employees fear speaking honestly?

- What small change could dramatically improve communication flow?

Summary and Key Takeaways

- Communication is the backbone of teamwork in public agencies.

- Supervisors must lead by example: honest, transparent, and consistent.

- Open and honest dialogue among employees builds psychological safety and efficiency.

- Common barriers—such as bureaucracy, hierarchy, silos, conflict, and technology—must be addressed proactively.

- Case studies demonstrate that small changes in communication habits can significantly enhance team effectiveness, particularly during crisis conditions.

"Clear communication is not a luxury in public service—it is the bridge between intention and trust."

4 FOSTERING TRUST AND COLLABORATION

Introduction

Trust is the invisible contract that enables collaboration. In government organizations, where teams operate under the scrutiny of citizens, auditors, and elected officials, trust is not just desirable—it is essential. Without trust, employees protect themselves, withhold ideas, and work in silos. With trust, they share information freely, take calculated risks, and collaborate to find solutions that enhance public service.

Supervisors serve as the architects of trust. Employees look to their leaders not only for instructions but for consistency, fairness, and credibility. Trust is built through small, repeated actions: keeping promises, communicating honestly, and treating every team member with respect and dignity. Once established, trust becomes the foundation for collaboration — the ability of individuals to align their skills, knowledge, and energy toward shared goals.

This chapter examines how supervisors can foster trust within their teams, promote collaboration across roles and departments, and manage conflict in a manner that strengthens rather than weakens relationships. We will examine strategies that supervisors can implement immediately, supported by case examples and exercises designed for public-sector settings.

Section 1: Building Trust Among Team Members and with the Supervisor

Trust is earned, not granted. In government teams, where employees often have long tenure and strong opinions about leadership, supervisors cannot assume trust automatically comes with the position. Instead, they must demonstrate trustworthiness through consistent behavior.

How Supervisors Build Trust

1. **Consistency** – Employees pay close attention to whether supervisors are consistent in applying rules, enforcing standards, and delivering on promises. A supervisor who disciplines one employee for tardiness but ignores the same behavior in another quickly loses credibility.

2. **Transparency** – Employees respect leaders who share information openly, especially about challenges and setbacks. If budgets are tight or priorities have shifted, honesty builds credibility. Concealing information often leads to rumors and mistrust.

3. **Fairness** – Perceptions of favoritism are toxic in government workplaces. Supervisors must ensure that recognition, workload, and opportunities are distributed fairly and equitably among employees.

4. **Follow-through** – Even small commitments matter. If a supervisor promises to bring up an employee's concern at the next management meeting, they must follow through and report back on it. Broken promises erode trust rapidly.

Trust Among Team Members

Supervisors must also cultivate trust between employees. This idea can be more challenging, as long-standing histories, generational divides, or union dynamics may foster suspicion. Strategies include:

- Encouraging transparency about workloads and deadlines.

- Creating opportunities for team members to learn about each other's roles.

- Setting clear expectations for respectful communication.
- Addressing breaches of trust immediately rather than allowing resentment to fester.

Supervisor's Tip

Trust grows in drops and leaks in buckets. Build it daily through small, consistent actions, and guard against careless behavior that can quickly drain it.

Quick Checklist: Building Trust

- Do I apply rules and standards consistently?
- Am I transparent about challenges and changes?
- Do I treat every team member with fairness and respect?
- Do I follow through on the commitments I make?
- Have I addressed breaches of trust promptly?

Reflection Box

- What is one action I can take this week to build trust with my team?
- Have I unintentionally signaled favoritism or inconsistency?
- How can I model vulnerability without undermining credibility?

Section 2: Encouraging Collaboration and Teamwork

Trust provides the foundation; collaboration is the structure built upon it. In public-sector organizations, collaboration often determines whether services are delivered effectively. A transportation team repairing streets must collaborate with utilities to avoid tearing up the same road twice. A public health team addressing a disease outbreak must collaborate with schools, clinics, and local governments to effectively manage the outbreak.

Why Collaboration Matters

Government problems are complex. Rarely can one employee, or even one department, solve them alone. Collaboration brings diverse perspectives and skills together, producing solutions that are more creative and more effective. For example, a city's homelessness initiative may require cooperation between housing, social services, law enforcement, and nonprofit partners.

How Supervisors Encourage Collaboration

1. **Clarify Shared Goals** – Employees must understand how their work contributes to the organization's overall mission and objectives. A supervisor should regularly emphasize the team's collective purpose rather than focusing solely on individual tasks.

2. **Design Collaborative Processes** – Encourage teamwork by structuring projects that require joint effort. For instance, assigning cross-functional task forces ensures employees work beyond silos.

3. **Recognize Collaborative Behavior** – Publicly highlight examples of employees helping one another. Recognition reinforces that collaboration is valued, not just individual achievement.

4. **Remove Barriers** – Collaboration is often hindered by conflicting priorities or miscommunication. Supervisors must identify and eliminate these barriers by coordinating schedules, clarifying responsibilities, or facilitating meetings between departments.

Did You Know?

Studies on organizational behavior indicate that employees in high-trust, collaborative environments experience 50% higher engagement levels compared to those in competitive or siloed workplaces.

Supervisor's Tip

Collaboration is not just about dividing work — it is about multiplying impact. Ensure your team views collaboration as the fastest path to success, not an added burden.

Quick Checklist: Encouraging Collaboration

- Have I clearly communicated the team's shared goals?

- Do my projects require collaboration, or do they isolate employees?

- Am I recognizing and rewarding collaborative behavior?

- Have I identified and removed barriers to teamwork?

Reflection Box

- Where does my team collaborate most effectively?

- Where do silos or competition undermine our mission?

- What is one step I can take this month to strengthen collaboration across roles?

Section 3: Resolving Conflicts and Promoting Harmony

Even in the most dedicated public-sector teams, conflict is inevitable. Employees bring different experiences, priorities, and personalities into the workplace. Add the pressures of limited budgets, high public expectations, and political oversight, and conflict can quickly escalate. For supervisors, the goal is not to eliminate conflict — which is impossible — but to channel it into productive dialogue that strengthens trust and fosters collaboration.

Sources of Conflict in Government Teams

1. **Resource Scarcity** – When budget cuts limit staff or equipment, employees may feel they are competing for resources.

2. **Role Overlap** – Ambiguity about responsibilities can lead to disputes over "who owns what."

3. **Generational and Cultural Differences** – Differing communication styles, work ethics, or values can create tension.

4. **Public Pressure** – External criticism may heighten internal stress, causing employees to turn on one another.

Supervisor Strategies for Conflict Resolution

- **Address Issues Early** – Small conflicts grow into large ones if ignored. Supervisors must address tension as soon as it emerges.

- **Separate People from Problems** – Remind employees that conflict is about issues, not personal worth.

- **Use Neutral Language** – Frame discussions around shared goals ("How can we ensure citizens get timely service?") rather than blame.

- **Encourage Perspective-Taking** – Asking, *"Help me understand your perspective,"* diffuses defensiveness and fosters empathy.

- **Establish Agreements** – Summarize the decisions made, clarify responsibilities, and follow up to ensure accountability.

- **Follow Up Consistently** – Conflict resolution is not complete at the end of the meeting. Supervisors should review agreements, monitor progress, and reinforce positive behaviors to facilitate resolution.

Supervisor's Tip

Conflict is not a sign of failure. It is a sign that people care enough to take an interest. The supervisor's job is to transform that energy into solutions.

Quick Checklist: Resolving Conflict

- Did I address the conflict promptly and directly?
- Did I focus on the issue rather than the personalities?
- Did I use language that encouraged problem-solving?
- Did I document agreements and follow up on them as needed?

Reflection Box

- What conflict have I avoided addressing, and why?
- How might addressing it now strengthen trust within my team?
- What new ground rules could help prevent future conflicts?

Case Snapshot: City Transportation and Public Works

A mid-sized city faced a significant infrastructure challenge. The transportation department planned to repave a main thoroughfare, while public works scheduled utility line replacements on the same road. Neither department communicated with the other until both projects were about to begin. The lack of coordination threatened to waste money and frustrate citizens by tearing up the road twice in the same month.

Recognizing the brewing conflict, a supervisor organized a joint meeting between the two teams. At first, the discussion was tense, with each side blaming the other. The supervisor shifted the tone by asking a unifying question: *"What solution best serves our citizens?"* That reframing moved the focus from blame to collaboration.

The teams agreed to coordinate schedules: utility work would be completed first, followed by repaving. The supervisor established weekly check-ins to ensure alignment and transparency. Citizens ultimately saw a single, coordinated project rather than two disruptive ones. Trust between departments improved, and the supervisor later institutionalized joint planning sessions for all future infrastructure projects.

This case illustrates how supervisors can utilize conflict as a catalyst for enhanced collaboration and teamwork. By redirecting the conversation toward shared goals, they turn potential failures into public wins.

Practice Exercise

Trust and Collaboration Workshop Activity

1. **Trust Mapping**: Ask each team member to write down one strength they see in another colleague anonymously. Share results in a group discussion to highlight mutual respect.

2. **Collaboration Challenge**: Assign a small project that requires cross-role cooperation (e.g., designing a new citizen feedback process). Debrief on what helped collaboration and what hindered it.

3. **Conflict Role-Play**: Present a fictional scenario (e.g., two employees disagree about who should handle citizen complaints)—role-play resolution strategies, focusing on

separating issues from personalities.

Reflection Questions

- How do I currently handle conflict in my team?

- Do my employees trust me to resolve issues fairly and equitably?

- What practices could I introduce to strengthen collaboration across departments?

- How will I measure whether trust is increasing over time?

Summary and Key Takeaways

- Trust is the foundation of all effective teamwork in the public sector. Supervisors build it through consistency, transparency, fairness, and follow-through.

- Collaboration requires intentional effort: clarifying shared goals, designing joint projects, recognizing cooperative behavior, and removing barriers.

- Conflict is inevitable but manageable. When addressed promptly and constructively, it can strengthen relationships and improve outcomes.

- Supervisors who focus on trust and collaboration not only improve internal morale but also enhance the quality of service delivered to citizens.

"Trust is the soil where collaboration grows. Without it, teamwork withers; with it, anything is possible."

5 LEVERAGING INDIVIDUAL STRENGTHS AND DIVERSITY

Introduction

Every government team comprises individuals who bring unique skills, experiences, and perspectives to their work. Some are natural problem-solvers, others excel at building relationships, and still others shine in technical expertise. When supervisors recognize and harness these strengths, teams become more than the sum of their parts.

At the same time, public-sector teams are diverse not only in ability but also in demographics, tenure, and personal backgrounds. Diversity can be a powerful driver of innovation, but it requires intentional leadership to move beyond surface-level acknowledgment. Supervisors must learn to build inclusive environments where differences are valued, equity is prioritized, and collaboration is strengthened through varied perspectives.

This chapter examines how supervisors can recognize and celebrate individual strengths, foster inclusivity, and leverage diversity as a source of creativity and innovation. It offers practical strategies to help government supervisors transform differences into assets that improve performance and strengthen service to the public.

Section 1: Recognizing and Appreciating Individual Strengths

Employees who utilize their strengths on a daily basis are more engaged, productive, and satisfied. In government agencies, where employees may feel constrained by bureaucracy, recognizing strengths allows supervisors to tap into hidden talents that standard job descriptions often overlook.

For example, in a county clerk's office, one employee may excel in detail-oriented tasks like proofreading documents, while another thrives in high-pressure situations at the customer service desk. By aligning responsibilities with strengths, supervisors can reduce errors, increase efficiency, and improve morale.

How to Identify Strengths

Supervisors can use both formal and informal methods:

- **Observation** – Notice when employees are energized or take initiative.

- **Conversations** – Ask employees directly about the tasks they enjoy the most and feel confident in.

- **Assessments** – Tools like Clifton Strengths or DiSC can provide structured insights into individual talents.

- **Peer Feedback** – Team members often see strengths in one another that supervisors might miss.

Practical Example

A supervisor in a city call center noticed that one employee had an extraordinary ability to calm angry citizens, while another excelled in navigating complex databases. The supervisor reassigned responsibilities, so the first employee handled escalated calls, and the second managed system troubleshooting. The result was faster resolutions and reduced stress for the entire team.

Supervisor's Tip

Please do not assume that employees want to keep doing what they are best at. Strengths should guide assignments, but variety and growth opportunities prevent stagnation.

Quick Checklist: Recognizing Strengths

- Have I identified which tasks energize my employees versus those that drain them?

- Do I regularly ask employees what parts of their job they enjoy most?

- Have I explored strengths assessments to deepen understanding?

- Do I celebrate strengths publicly so the team sees each other's value?

Reflection Box

- What are the top three strengths of each of my team members?

- Am I fully utilizing those strengths in current assignments?

- How could better alignment of strengths improve our services?

Section 2: Promoting Inclusivity and Diversity within Teams

Diversity in public-sector teams extends beyond visible traits, such as race, gender, or age. It includes differences in education, work experience, communication styles, problem-solving approaches, and even tenure in government service. Inclusivity means ensuring that all these perspectives are not only present but also valued and integrated into the decision-making process.

Why Inclusivity Matters

In government, inclusivity is tied directly to legitimacy. Citizens expect that agencies reflect and respect the diversity of the communities they serve. A team that values inclusivity is more likely to design services that meet varied needs, anticipate community concerns, and build trust with stakeholders.

Strategies for Supervisors

1. **Set Clear Expectations** – Communicate that respect and equity are non-negotiable cultural values.

2. **Model Inclusive Behavior** – Give credit fairly, invite quiet voices into discussions, and intervene when exclusionary behavior occurs.

3. **Facilitate Equitable Participation** – In meetings, ensure that a few voices do not dominate discussions. Rotate who leads agenda items.

4. **Provide Training and Development** – Offer opportunities to learn about cultural competency, unconscious bias, and inclusive communication.

5. **Celebrate Diversity** – Recognize and honor the cultural events, traditions, and perspectives that are relevant to your workforce and community.

Practical Example

A supervisor in a state human services agency realized that younger employees were often hesitant to share ideas in meetings dominated by long-tenured staff. She instituted a "round-robin" discussion format where every participant shared at least one suggestion before the meeting ended. This simple shift created space for new voices and uncovered innovative solutions that had been hidden by hierarchy.

Did You Know?

Research shows that teams with higher levels of diversity are **45% more likely** to report market share growth in the private sector. In government, this translates into innovation and stronger service delivery for diverse communities.

Supervisor's Tip

Inclusivity does not happen by accident. It occurs when supervisors intentionally create space for every voice to be heard.

Quick Checklist: Promoting Inclusivity

- Do all employees feel their voices are valued and heard?
- Do I model fairness in giving credit and opportunities?
- Have I structured meetings to ensure balanced participation and

engagement?

- Do I celebrate the diverse backgrounds represented on my team?

Reflection Box

- Whose voices are most dominant in my team?

- Whose perspectives are often missing or overlooked?

- What steps can I take this month to ensure greater inclusivity?

Section 3: Leveraging Diversity to Drive Innovation and Creativity

Diversity becomes a true asset when it moves beyond representation and into application. Government teams face complex challenges — aging infrastructure, public health crises, community safety, and environmental sustainability — that rarely have simple solutions. To tackle these issues, agencies must draw from the full range of perspectives within their workforce.

The Link Between Diversity and Innovation

Different perspectives generate more ideas, highlight risks earlier, and uncover opportunities that uniform groups might miss. A city planning team that includes engineers, community organizers, and environmental specialists is far more likely to design resilient and equitable projects than one dominated by a single viewpoint.

Supervisor's Role in Leveraging Diversity

- **Facilitate Idea Generation** – Use brainstorming sessions that encourage contributions from every team member. Techniques such as "round-robin" sharing or anonymous digital input ensure diverse perspectives surface.

- **Encourage Constructive Debate** – Diverse teams may disagree more, but when managed respectfully, conflict sparks creativity. Supervisors should emphasize debate as a means of finding solutions, rather than resorting to personal attacks.

- **Value Different Work Styles** – Some employees think best in group discussions, while others need quiet reflection. Offering multiple avenues for input respects these differences and enhances overall innovation.

- **Highlight Community Impact** – Show employees how their diverse input leads to better outcomes for citizens. Linking creativity to public benefit increases motivation and pride.

Did You Know?

Public-sector studies indicate that citizen satisfaction increases significantly when government services are designed with input from diverse employee groups, particularly in areas of health, housing, and education.

Supervisor's Tip

Innovation does not come from the loudest voice — it comes from the broadest range of voices. Ensure that every perspective has a chance to influence the outcome.

Quick Checklist: Leveraging Diversity for Innovation

- Have I created forums where all employees can share ideas?
- Do I treat disagreement as an opportunity rather than a threat?
- Do I adapt processes to respect different communication and work styles?
- Have I linked diversity of input to improved outcomes?

Reflection Box

- What is one example where diverse perspectives improved my team's work?
- Where do I need to create more space for underrepresented voices?
- How can I better communicate the value of diversity to my team?
- Am I creating opportunities for every team member to contribute their perspective, not just the most vocal?

Case Snapshot: State Department of Environmental Services

A state environmental services department faced a challenge: an increase in complaints about water quality from rural communities. Initial discussions among senior engineers centered on technical solutions, such as upgrading treatment facilities. However, a supervisor recognized the need for broader input and assembled a diverse task force including engineers, community outreach staff, field inspectors, and residents.

The engineers provided technical expertise, but community staff highlighted barriers to access, such as residents' distrust of government agencies. Field inspectors identified patterns in data collection that engineers had overlooked. Together, the group designed a two-pronged solution: targeted infrastructure upgrades paired with a citizen education campaign led by local staff familiar with community concerns.

The result was not only improved water quality but also strengthened public trust in the department. Citizens reported greater satisfaction because they felt their voices shaped the solution. The supervisor later reflected that diversity did not slow the process — it made the solution more complete and more legitimate.

Practice Exercise

Strengths and Diversity Mapping

1. Ask each team member to identify their top three strengths in the workplace.

2. Collect responses and create a team "strengths map" showing where skills are concentrated and where gaps exist.

3. During a team meeting, discuss how these strengths complement one another.

4. Next, ask employees to share a perspective or experience (professional or personal) they believe adds unique value to the team.

5. Reflect as a group on how to better leverage these strengths and perspectives in upcoming projects.

Reflection Questions

- Do I know the top strengths of each of my team members?

- Have I created opportunities for diverse perspectives to influence decisions?

- What barriers prevent full inclusion in my team, and how can I remove them?

- How can I determine whether diversity is resulting in improved outcomes for citizens?

Summary and Key Takeaways

- Recognizing and aligning individual strengths improves engagement, efficiency, and morale.

- Inclusivity ensures that all voices are valued, particularly in hierarchical or unionized government environments.

- Diversity drives innovation when supervisors create structures that foster constructive dialogue and respect diverse work styles.

- Case studies demonstrate that diverse perspectives improve both the quality of solutions and citizen satisfaction with public services.

- Supervisors must be intentional in harnessing strengths and diversity — it does not happen automatically.

"Diversity is not just about who is in the room; it is about ensuring every voice shapes the work. Strengths and perspectives, when combined, create solutions greater than any one person could imagine."

6 MOTIVATING AND EMPOWERING TEAM MEMBERS

Introduction

In government organizations, motivation is often misunderstood. While the private sector may use bonuses, promotions, or profit-sharing to drive performance, public-sector employees are motivated by different levers: a sense of service to the community, fairness, recognition, and meaningful work. Supervisors must understand these unique motivators and create an environment that empowers employees to perform at their best.

Empowerment goes hand in hand with motivation. Supervisors cannot simply inspire employees with words; they must also grant the autonomy, authority, and trust that allow individuals to act on their motivation. When supervisors delegate effectively and provide the resources and recognition employees need, they unleash energy that benefits both the team and the citizens they serve.

This chapter examines the psychology of motivation in government teams, the impact of delegation and autonomy, and the role of feedback and recognition in sustaining high performance. It provides practical strategies for supervisors who want to move beyond compliance and cultivate genuine commitment.

Section 1: Understanding Motivation in the Public Sector

Government employees often enter public service with a strong sense of civic duty. They value stability, fairness, and the opportunity to contribute to the common good. Nevertheless, over time, motivation can erode under the weight of bureaucracy, limited resources, or a lack of recognition. Supervisors must actively nurture motivation by connecting daily tasks to meaningful outcomes.

Intrinsic vs. Extrinsic Motivation

- **Intrinsic motivation** is from within: the satisfaction of solving problems, the pride of serving, and the joy of mastering a skill.

- **Extrinsic motivation** originates from external rewards, such as pay, promotions, or recognition.

In public service, intrinsic motivators are often more powerful than extrinsic ones. A DMV employee may not receive a bonus for processing more licenses. Still, they may feel pride in reducing wait times for frustrated citizens—supervisors who emphasize the impact of service tap into deeper motivation than those who focus solely on compliance.

Supervisor Strategies for Motivation

1. **Connect Work to Impact** – Remind employees how their efforts improve citizens' lives. For example, sanitation workers are not just collecting trash; they are protecting public health and community pride.

2. **Set Achievable Goals** – Motivation thrives when employees see progress. Break large projects into smaller milestones and celebrate each achievement.

3. **Encourage Mastery** – Offer training and skill development. Employees who grow feel invested in their work.

4. **Recognize Effort as Well as Results** – Not every task yields immediate success. Recognizing effort helps maintain high morale even during setbacks.

Did You Know?

Research shows that public-sector employees who feel their work benefits the community are **30% more engaged** than those who view their tasks as purely administrative in nature.

Supervisor's Tip

Motivation is not something you give employees — it is something you unlock by connecting their work to a sense of meaning.

Quick Checklist: Motivating Employees

- Have I explained how this task benefits the community?
- Are goals broken down into achievable steps?
- Am I providing training or growth opportunities?
- Do I recognize effort, not just outcomes?

Reflection Box

- What motivates each of my employees the most?
- How often do I link daily tasks to the impact on citizens?
- What training or growth opportunities can I provide this year?

Section 2: Empowering Team Members through Delegation and Autonomy

Motivation without empowerment quickly turns into frustration. Employees who feel inspired but constrained by micromanagement or a lack of authority will tend to disengage. Supervisors must pair motivation with real opportunities for autonomy.

Why Empowerment Matters

Empowerment builds ownership. Employees who feel trusted make better decisions, act proactively, and take pride in outcomes. In government settings, empowerment also builds resilience. When supervisors cannot be present for every decision, empowered employees ensure that services run smoothly.

The Art of Delegation

Delegation is not just about assigning tasks — it is about transferring authority and responsibility while providing the necessary support for success. Effective delegation requires:

1. **Choosing the Right Task** – Not all tasks can be delegated.

Select those that match the employee's skills and offer growth opportunities.

2. **Providing Clear Expectations** – Define outcomes, deadlines, and boundaries. Avoid vague instructions.

3. **Granting Authority** – Empower employees to make necessary decisions within the scope of the task.

4. **Offering Support** – Provide resources and check in periodically without micromanaging.

5. **Holding Accountable** – Review outcomes, provide feedback, and recognize accomplishments.

Example

In a city housing department, a supervisor delegated responsibility for community workshops to a mid-level employee. Consider a situation where a project manager delegates the responsibility of organizing a community event to an employee with strong organizational skills.

The manager clearly outlines the goals, provides necessary resources, and empowers the employee to make decisions regarding logistics and outreach. As a result, the employee not only delivers a successful event but also develops confidence and new skills, illustrating how thoughtful delegation fosters both professional growth and effective outcomes.

She gave the employee authority to design the agenda, coordinate logistics, and represent the department at neighborhood meetings. By trusting her employee, the supervisor not only freed her own time but also built leadership capacity within the team.

Supervisor's Tip

Delegation without authority is just dumping work. True empowerment requires both responsibility and the freedom to act.

Autonomy and Innovation

When employees feel empowered, they are more likely to innovate and drive new ideas. For example, a team of maintenance workers given autonomy to schedule their own routes may find faster and more efficient ways to complete tasks than if a supervisor dictated every step.

Quick Checklist: Empowering Employees

- Have I matched tasks to the right employee's strengths?
- Did I define outcomes and boundaries clearly?
- Have I granted absolute authority, not just responsibility?
- Am I supporting without micromanaging?
- Did I provide feedback and recognition after the task was completed?

Reflection Box

- Do my employees feel trusted to make decisions?
- Which tasks could I delegate more effectively this month?
- How could greater autonomy improve our service delivery?

Section 3: Providing Constructive Feedback and Recognition

Feedback and recognition are the fuel that sustains motivation and empowerment over time. Without feedback, employees cannot improve their performance. Without recognition, they may feel invisible. In the public sector, where promotions and monetary rewards are often limited, the supervisor's role in providing meaningful feedback and recognition becomes even more critical.

The Power of Constructive Feedback

Constructive feedback helps employees identify what they are doing well and where they need to make adjustments. For feedback to be effective, it should be:

- **Timely** – Provide feedback promptly, not months later during annual reviews.

- **Specific** – General statements like "good job" lack impact. Specific feedback, such as "Your clear explanation helped calm that citizen," reinforces desired behaviors.

- **Balanced** – Highlight strengths before addressing areas of improvement. This keeps feedback from feeling punitive.

- **Actionable** – Provide concrete steps employees can take to improve.

Recognition as Motivation

Recognition affirms value and strengthens morale. It can be formal (awards, certificates, public announcements) or informal (verbal praise, handwritten notes, thank-you emails). In government, where employees may feel overlooked, recognition communicates that their efforts are seen and appreciated.

Practical Example

A supervisor in a state licensing agency began writing short "spotlight notes" each week, recognizing one employee's contribution — from handling a demanding customer with grace to streamlining a form. The notes were shared in team meetings. Employees reported feeling more valued, and morale improved significantly without any additional budget.

Supervisor's Tip

Recognition does not have to cost money. A simple, genuine thank-you can be more motivating than a formal award.

Quick Checklist: Feedback and Recognition

- Do I provide feedback in real-time, beyond annual reviews?

- Do I regularly recognize effort, not just outcomes?

- Have I created formal and informal recognition opportunities?

Reflection Box

- How often do I give constructive feedback to team members?

- Do employees feel appreciated for their work?

- What new recognition practice can I implement this month?

Case Snapshot: Municipal Library System

An extensive municipal library struggled with staff morale. Employees felt their contributions went unnoticed, and supervisors focused only on errors. Turnover among younger staff was rising.

A new branch supervisor decided to shift the culture by introducing empowerment and recognition. She delegated programming decisions to frontline staff, allowing them to design community events. She also began ending each weekly staff meeting with "shout-outs," inviting employees to recognize one another's contributions.

Within months, the atmosphere changed. Employees reported feeling trusted and valued. Innovative programs emerged — from digital literacy workshops to children's storytelling events — that drew record attendance. By combining delegation with consistent recognition, the supervisor transformed the library into a vibrant hub for the community.

Practice Exercise

Delegation and Recognition Planning

1. List three tasks currently on your plate that could be delegated to team members.

2. For each task, identify the employee best suited based on strengths.

3. Define outcomes, boundaries, and authority for each delegated task clearly and concisely.

4. Create a recognition plan: How will you acknowledge both the effort and results of the delegated tasks?

5. Implement one delegation/recognition cycle within the next 30 days.

Reflection Questions

- Do I strike a balance between constructive feedback and recognition?

- Have I created opportunities for employees to feel empowered, not micromanaged?

- How can I tailor my motivational strategies to meet the diverse needs of my employees?

- What practices can I implement this quarter to sustain motivation across the team?

Summary and Key Takeaways

- Motivation in public-sector teams thrives when employees see the impact of their work on the community.

- Empowerment requires supervisors to delegate not only tasks but also responsibility and authority.

- Constructive feedback must be timely, specific, balanced, and actionable.

- Recognition — both formal and informal — is a powerful motivator, especially where financial rewards are limited.

- Supervisors who integrate motivation, empowerment, feedback, and recognition create resilient, engaged teams that deliver stronger results to the public.

"Empowerment is the highest form of motivation. When people are trusted, recognized, and equipped, they rise to the challenge."

7 Leading Teams Through Change

Introduction

Change is a defining characteristic of government work. Policies shift with new administrations, budgets fluctuate in response to legislative priorities, and public expectations evolve in reaction to crises and technological advancements. For supervisors, the challenge is not whether change will occur, but how to guide teams through it effectively.

In the public sector, change often arrives with added complexity, including lengthy approval processes, union agreements, public scrutiny, and political influences. These realities can make employees skeptical, anxious, or resistant to change. However, with skilled leadership, change can become an opportunity for growth, innovation, and stronger service delivery.

Supervisors who succeed in leading change do more than issue directives; they translate change into meaning, reduce uncertainty, and build confidence in the path forward. This chapter examines the impact of change on teams, provides strategies for leading through organizational shifts, and offers tools to help employees adapt and thrive in evolving environments.

Section 1: Understanding the Impact of Change on Teams

Change affects individuals differently, but common patterns emerge in team behavior. Supervisors who anticipate these patterns are better prepared to respond.

Emotional Responses to Change

Employees often experience a cycle of emotions when confronted with change:

- **Shock and Denial** – Initial disbelief or hope that the change will not last.

- **Frustration and Resistance** – Fear of losing familiar routines, roles, or status.

- **Exploration** – Gradual testing of new ways of working.

- **Acceptance and Commitment** – Integration of new practices into daily routines.

For example, when a state agency introduces a new case management system, some employees may resist training sessions, insisting the old system worked fine. Over time, however, with support and encouragement, they begin to see the benefits of faster reporting and fewer errors.

Practical Impact on Teams

Beyond emotional reactions, change also carries tangible effects on the day-to-day functioning of teams, often disrupting stability and reshaping how work gets done

Change often creates:

- **Uncertainty** – Employees wonder how changes will affect their jobs.

- **Productivity dips** – Energy shifts from routine tasks to learning new processes.

- **Conflict** – Tension arises when some employees embrace change while others resist.

- **Turnover** – Employees unwilling to adapt may leave, taking institutional knowledge with them.

Supervisor's Tip

Do not mistake resistance for laziness. Resistance usually signals fear, confusion, or lack of information. Address the root cause and behavior.

Quick Checklist: Recognizing Change Impact

- Have I acknowledged the emotional side of change, not just the technical side?

- Do I know where uncertainty is highest in my team?

- Am I monitoring for dips in productivity or morale?

- Have I identified employees who need support in transitions?

Reflection Box

- How has my team responded to change in the past?

- Which employees are most likely to struggle with uncertainty?

- How can I be empathic while still moving the team forward?

Section 2: Strategies for Leading Through Organizational Change

Effective change leadership requires more than delivering memos. Supervisors must actively guide employees through the transition, striking a balance between honesty, empathy, and structure.

Communicate Early and Often

Silence breeds rumors. Even when details are incomplete, supervisors should share what is known, acknowledge uncertainties, and commit to updates. Employees would rather hear, *"We don't have all the answers yet, but here is what we know so far,"* than nothing at all.

Provide Context and Meaning

Explain the "why" behind the change. If a city department is reorganizing to improve efficiency, it should clearly connect the change to enhanced citizen service, reduced wait times, or improved resource utilization. Employees who understand the bigger picture are more likely to accept short-term discomfort.

Involve Employees in the Process

Employees tend to resist changes imposed on them, but they are more likely to support changes they help shape. Involve staff in pilot programs, feedback sessions, or process redesigns to gather their input and insights. Their insights not only improve implementation but also increase buy-in.

Acknowledge Losses

Change often involves loss of routines, colleagues, or control. Supervisors should acknowledge these losses openly rather than pretending they do not exist. A simple statement, such as *"I know this transition is hard and that we will miss some of the old ways,"* builds trust.

Create Stability Amid Change

Highlight what is not changing. For instance, even if reporting lines shift, the team's commitment to serving citizens remains the same. Stability reassures employees that change is not chaos.

Model Adaptability

Employees watch how supervisors react. Leaders who remain calm, curious, and flexible send a powerful message that change is manageable and can be navigated effectively. Leaders who panic or resist undermine confidence.

Did You Know?

Studies show that organizations with strong change communication are **3.5 times more likely** to outperform peers in implementing new initiatives.

Supervisor's Tip

Employees do not need supervisors to be perfect during change — they need them to be present, honest, and steady.

Quick Checklist: Leading Change

- Have I explained the "why" behind the change clearly?
- Am I communicating regularly, even when details are not yet

complete?

- Have I involved employees in shaping or implementing the change?

- Have I acknowledged what employees may be losing?

- Am I modeling adaptability and resilience?

Reflection Box

- How do I personally react to change, and what example does that set for others?

- Have I been honest about uncertainties, or do I avoid difficult conversations?

- What steps can I take to increase employee involvement in this transition?

Section 3: Helping Teams Adapt and Thrive in a Changing Environment

Change leadership is not just about guiding employees through disruption — it is about equipping them to thrive in the new reality. Supervisors who invest in adaptation skills build resilient teams capable of handling future transitions with confidence.

1. **Normalize Adaptability**

   Supervisors should communicate that change is not an exception but a natural part of government work. By framing adaptability as a core competency, supervisors help employees shift from resisting change to expecting and preparing for it.

2. **Provide Training and Resources**

   New systems, processes, or policies often necessitate the acquisition of new skills. A supervisor who ensures timely training reduces frustration and builds confidence. Even modest investments, such as peer coaching or quick-reference guides, can help employees adapt more smoothly to new situations.

Celebrate Small Wins

Acknowledging progress helps maintain high morale during periods of transition. If a team successfully meets the first deadline under a new system, celebrate that milestone. Recognition builds momentum and signals that the team is on the right track.

Support Emotional Well-Being

Change is stressful. Supervisors can encourage open conversations about concerns, provide flexibility when possible, and direct employees to employee assistance programs or wellness resources. Supportive supervisors remind employees they are not navigating change alone.

Reinforce Core Purpose

Even amid transition, public-sector teams share a constant mission: serving citizens. Reminding employees of this purpose provides stability and anchors motivation.

Supervisor's Tip

People are more adaptable than they realize. Show them their progress, celebrate their resilience, and remind them that change reveals strengths they did not know they had.

Quick Checklist: Helping Teams Adapt

- Am I framing adaptability as a core skill?

- Have I provided training and resources to support the development of new skills?

- Do I celebrate progress during transitions?

- Am I attentive to the emotional impact of change?

- Have I connected the change to our enduring purpose of service?

Reflection Box

- What adaptation skills does my team need most at this time?

- How can I reduce stress and increase confidence during this transition?

- How will I know my team is thriving, not just surviving, through this change?

Case Snapshot: City Finance Department

A city finance department faced a sudden mandate: transition to a new statewide accounting system within six months. Employees, already burdened with annual budget preparation, felt overwhelmed and resistant to change.

The supervisor approached the challenge by breaking the change into manageable steps. She secured training sessions for staff, created a buddy system pairing tech-savvy employees with those less comfortable, and held weekly progress check-ins to celebrate achievements. She acknowledged frustrations openly, reminding the team that the work was difficult but necessary.

The result was a smoother transition than expected. Employees gained confidence in using the system, errors decreased, and the department met the state's deadline. More importantly, staff later reflected that they felt "carried" through the change rather than "pushed." The supervisor's approach turned resistance into resilience.

Practice Exercise

Change Mapping for Supervisors

1. Identify a recent or upcoming change your team is facing.

2. Map the potential impacts: What will employees gain? What will they lose?

3. List specific actions you will take to:

   o Communicate the "why" behind the change.

   o Involve employees in shaping the process.

   o Provide training or resources to support adaptation.

o   Recognize and celebrate progress.

4. Share the map with your team to ensure transparency and facilitate feedback.

Reflection Questions

- How do I currently support my team in adapting to change?

- Do I provide both technical support (training) and emotional support (empathy)?

- How can I better celebrate progress during transitions?

- What strategies from this chapter can I implement in the next 30 days?

Summary and Key Takeaways

- Change is constant in government and requires intentional leadership.

- Employees often experience emotional stages of change: denial, resistance, exploration, and acceptance.

- Supervisors lead effectively by communicating early, providing context, involving employees, and modeling adaptability.

- Teams thrive in change when supervisors normalize adaptability, provide training, celebrate progress, and support well-being.

- Real-world examples demonstrate that supportive, structured leadership can transform resistance into resilience.

"Change does not weaken teams — it reveals their strength. With steady leadership, what begins as resistance can end as resilience."

8 DEVELOPING LEADERSHIP SKILLS IN SUPERVISORS

Introduction

In government organizations, supervisors are often promoted due to their technical expertise or long tenure, rather than their proven leadership skills. A skilled accountant may become the head of a finance team, or a veteran field inspector may be elevated to supervise others. While technical knowledge is important, leadership requires a different set of competencies — the ability to inspire, guide, and develop people.

Without leadership development, supervisors risk defaulting to habits of control, compliance, or avoidance. This can lead to disengagement, conflict, and missed opportunities for innovation. Nevertheless, when supervisors are equipped with leadership skills, they become catalysts for higher performance, stronger morale, and improved public service.

This chapter explores the qualities that define effective supervisors in the public sector, strategies for providing leadership training and development, and the importance of self-reflection in continuous growth. Supervisors who invest in their leadership journey not only improve their own performance but also elevate the entire workforce.

Section 1: Identifying Essential Leadership Qualities for Supervisors

Not all leadership qualities are equal. In public-sector environments, where fairness, accountability, and service are paramount, certain qualities are essential for effective supervisors.

1. Integrity

Supervisors must model ethical behavior. In government, where public trust is fragile, integrity is non-negotiable. Employees look to supervisors for signals about what is acceptable. A single lapse in honesty can erode credibility across the team.

2. Communication

Clear, honest, and consistent communication is the foundation of leadership. Supervisors must be able to translate policy into action, provide feedback, and listen to employee concerns. Strong communicators reduce misunderstandings and build trust.

3. Emotional Intelligence

Supervisors with emotional intelligence can recognize and manage their own emotions while understanding and responding to the emotions of others. This skill is especially critical in conflict resolution, performance conversations, and change management.

4. Fairness and Consistency

Employees are quick to notice favoritism or double standards. Fairness ensures credibility, while consistency reinforces stability in high-pressure environments.

Vision and Strategic Thinking

Even at the frontline level, supervisors must connect daily work to larger agency goals. Visionary supervisors inspire employees by showing how their tasks contribute to the public good.

6. Adaptability

Public-sector supervisors operate in an environment of constant change — political shifts, policy reforms, budget cuts. Adaptability allows them to pivot while keeping the team focused.

7. Commitment to Employee Growth

Great supervisors invest in their employees' development. They see leadership not as control but as empowerment, creating opportunities for growth and learning.

Did You Know?

Studies show that employees who rate their supervisors highly on integrity and fairness are **70% more likely** to report feeling engaged and committed to their organization.

Supervisor's Tip

Leadership is not about a title — it is about influence. The way you act daily shapes how others respond, far more than your position on the organizational chart.

Quick Checklist: Essential Qualities

- Do I consistently demonstrate integrity in my decisions?
- Is my communication clear, honest, and consistent?
- Am I aware of the emotions driving my team's behavior?
- Do employees trust me to be fair and consistent in my decisions?
- Have I connected team tasks to a larger vision?
- Do I adapt quickly to new directives or conditions?
- Am I actively supporting the growth of my employees?

Reflection Box

- Which leadership qualities are my strongest?
- Which qualities need the most development?
- What steps can I take to strengthen my leadership presence this year?

Section 2: Providing Leadership Training and Development

Opportunities

Leadership does not come naturally to everyone — but it can be developed. Public-sector organizations that invest in leadership development for supervisors see improvements in employee engagement, retention, and performance.

Formal Training Programs

Many government agencies now offer structured programs:

- **Leadership academies** that provide multi-month training in communication, conflict resolution, and strategic thinking.

- **Supervisor boot camps** focus on practical skills, including performance management, delegation, and compliance.

- **Mentorship programs** pair new supervisors with experienced leaders for guidance and support.

On-the-Job Development

Not all development happens in classrooms. Supervisors grow through:

- **Stretch Assignments** – Leading a cross-department project or pilot initiative.

- **Job Rotations** – Spending time in another department to broaden perspective.

- **Acting Assignments** – Temporarily filling in for higher-level leaders.

- **Shadowing Opportunities** – Spending time observing senior leaders or peers in different roles to gain insight into decision-making styles, leadership tactics, and organizational dynamics.

Peer Learning

Supervisors benefit from sharing their experiences. Peer networks, roundtables, and communities of practice offer safe spaces for discussing challenges and solutions.

Leveraging Technology

E-learning platforms, webinars, and microlearning modules make leadership training more accessible, especially in resource-limited agencies. Supervisors can engage in ongoing learning without leaving their teams understaffed.

Supervisor's Tip

Leadership development is not a one-time workshop — it is a continuous process. Encourage your agency to invest in ongoing opportunities and take personal responsibility for your growth.

Quick Checklist: Leadership Development Opportunities

- Have I participated in formal training to strengthen my leadership skills?

- Do I seek out stretch assignments to expand my experience?

- Am I connected to a peer network of supervisors for shared learning and professional development?

- Have I explored opportunities to continue my development?

- Do I encourage my employees to pursue growth alongside me?

Reflection Box

- What formal training opportunities are currently available to me?

- What informal opportunities (projects, mentoring, peer learning) can I pursue?

- How can I model continuous growth for my team?

Section 3: Encouraging Self-Reflection and Continuous Growth

Leadership development is not only about external training or formal programs. The most powerful growth often comes through **self-reflection** — the practice of examining one's actions, decisions, and impact on others. Supervisors who build the habit of reflection become more self-aware, adaptable, and effective.

The Role of Self-Awareness

Self-awareness is the foundation of emotional intelligence. Supervisors who recognize their strengths and weaknesses are less defensive when receiving feedback and more intentional in their leadership choices. A self-aware supervisor might realize, *"I tend to avoid conflict. I need to be more proactive in addressing issues before they escalate."*

Reflection Practices

- **Journaling** – Writing briefly each week about successes, challenges, and lessons learned.

- **After-Action Reviews** – Reflecting after major projects: What worked? What did not? What should we do differently?

- **Feedback Seeking** – Asking employees and peers for candid input. A simple question, such as *"What is one thing I could do to support you better?"* can provide powerful insights.

- **Quiet Time** – Taking even 10 minutes of uninterrupted reflection at the end of the day to consider leadership decisions.

Commitment to Lifelong Learning

Government work is constantly evolving, with new policies, technologies, and changing community needs. Supervisors must commit to ongoing growth, treating leadership as a lifelong journey rather than a destination. Reading leadership literature, attending conferences, and learning from peers keep skills fresh and relevant.

Supervisor's Tip

Reflection without action is just nostalgia. Apply what you learn about yourself to make minor yet meaningful adjustments in your leadership.

Quick Checklist: Self-Reflection and Growth

- Do I regularly set aside time for self-reflection?

- Have I sought recent feedback from my employees or peers?

- Do I view leadership as a continuous journey, or a fixed skill set?

- Am I modeling growth for my team by being open to learning and growth?

Reflection Box

- What is one leadership habit I need to change?

- How can I hold myself accountable for continuous growth?

- What example am I setting for my employees about learning?

Case Snapshot: State Department of Transportation

A state Department of Transportation recognized that many of its supervisors had technical expertise but limited leadership training. Employee surveys revealed frustrations with inconsistent supervision, poor communication, and inadequate support.

The agency launched a "Supervisor Development Initiative." Supervisors attended workshops on communication, conflict resolution, and coaching. Each was also assigned a leadership journal, where they recorded weekly reflections on their successes and challenges. Supervisors shared excerpts during peer roundtables, building a culture of openness and mutual support.

One supervisor later admitted that reflection changed his leadership style more than any workshop: *"Writing down my patterns made me see that I was always avoiding tough conversations. Once I realized that, I could change."* Over time, employee engagement scores improved, turnover declined, and the agency built a stronger bench of leaders ready for future challenges.

Practice Exercise

Leadership Self-Reflection Plan

1. Select a reflection method (journal, after-action review, or feedback-seeking).

2. Commit to practicing it weekly for one month.

3. At the end of the month, write a summary of what you learned about your leadership habits.

4. Identify one change you will implement in the next 30 days.

5. Share your plan with a trusted peer or mentor to hold yourself accountable.

Reflection Questions

- Do I take time to reflect on my leadership, or do I move from task to task without pause?

- Have I asked my team for feedback on my leadership recently?

- What leadership skill or habit do I most want to strengthen this year?

- How can I integrate continuous growth into my leadership journey?

Summary and Key Takeaways

- Adequate supervision in government requires more than technical expertise — it necessitates leadership qualities such as integrity, effective communication, emotional intelligence, fairness, adaptability, and a commitment to employee growth.

- Leadership skills can be developed through both formal training (such as academies and boot camps) and informal opportunities (including stretch assignments and peer networks).

- Self-reflection and lifelong learning are essential for continuous growth. Supervisors who examine their actions and seek feedback adapt more quickly and lead with greater authenticity.

- Agencies that invest in supervisor leadership development strengthen employee engagement, reduce turnover, and improve service to citizens.

"Leadership is not a position you achieve; it is a practice you commit to. Growth begins the moment you choose to reflect and learn."

9 MANAGING PERFORMANCE AND ACCOUNTABILITY

Introduction

Accountability is one of the cornerstones of public service. Citizens expect government employees to use resources wisely, follow rules consistently, and deliver services fairly. Unlike private-sector organizations, where accountability is often measured by profits or customer satisfaction, government accountability extends to taxpayers, elected officials, auditors, and the broader community.

For supervisors, accountability begins at the team level. Employees must understand what is expected of them, know how their performance will be measured, and trust that evaluations will be fair. When accountability is lacking, teams drift, productivity declines, and public confidence erodes. However, when supervisors establish clear standards, monitor progress, and address performance issues promptly, they foster a culture of responsibility that enhances both the team and the agency's credibility.

This chapter examines how supervisors can establish clear expectations, effectively monitor and evaluate performance, and address underperformance in a manner that promotes fairness and growth. By mastering these skills, supervisors ensure their teams deliver consistent, high-quality service to the public.

Section 1: Setting Clear Expectations and Performance Standards

The Importance of Clarity

Employees cannot be accountable for what they do not understand. In many government agencies, job descriptions are outdated or unclear, leaving employees uncertain about their roles and responsibilities. Supervisors must bridge this gap by clearly defining expectations and performance standards.

Steps for Setting Expectations

1. **Define Responsibilities** – Clarify roles beyond what is written in job descriptions. Outline daily, weekly, and project-based duties in specific terms.

2. **Set Standards of Quality** – Describe not only *what* needs to be done but *how well* it should be done. For example, "Respond to citizen inquiries within 48 hours" provides a measurable standard.

3. **Align with Agency Goals** – Connect team expectations to broader organizational missions. A public works crew maintaining roads should view their work as part of ensuring safe and reliable transportation for the community.

4. **Communicate Consistently** – Expectations must be stated, reinforced in meetings, and documented in writing. Verbal instructions alone are easily forgotten or misunderstood.

5. **Involve Employees** – Ask for input when setting standards. Employees often know what is realistic and where improvements can be made.

Supervisor's Tip

Clear expectations reduce conflict. When employees know what success looks like, they spend less time guessing and more time delivering.

Quick Checklist: Setting Expectations

- Are job responsibilities clarified beyond old job descriptions?

- Have I defined both outcomes and quality standards?

- Are team expectations connected to agency goals?

- Have I communicated expectations in writing and reinforced them verbally?

- Did I involve employees in shaping standards?

Reflection Box

- Do my employees know exactly what is expected of them?

- Have I connected team expectations to the agency's mission?

- What expectations do I need to clarify this week?

Section 2: Monitoring and Evaluating Performance Effectively

Setting expectations is only the first step; supervisors must also monitor progress and provide feedback. In government, where accountability is under constant scrutiny, effective monitoring ensures that services meet standards and taxpayer resources are used responsibly.

Principles of Monitoring Performance

- **Consistency** – Apply the same monitoring methods across all employees to avoid perceptions of favoritism.

- **Transparency** – Be clear about how performance is being measured and why.

- **Frequency** – Monitoring should be ongoing, not reserved for annual reviews.

- **Balanced Approach** – Look for both strengths and areas of improvement.

Methods of Evaluation

1. **Direct Observation** – Supervisors spend time observing employees as they perform tasks. This process provides real insight into work habits and challenges.

2. **Performance Metrics** – Use measurable indicators, such as response times, error rates, or citizen satisfaction scores.

3. **Self-Assessment** – Ask employees to reflect on their performance. This assessment encourages ownership and often reveals insights supervisors might miss.

4. **Peer Input** – In collaborative environments, peer feedback can highlight teamwork strengths and weaknesses.

5. **Documentation Review** – Examine reports, case files, or completed projects for accuracy and quality.

Example

At a county human services office, supervisors implemented a monthly performance dashboard that tracked case resolution times, accuracy rates, and citizen feedback. Sharing the dashboard with the team increased transparency and motivated employees to collaborate and improve.

Providing Evaluative Feedback

Evaluations are not judgments but guidance. Effective supervisors:

- Start with positives before addressing concerns.
- Use specific examples, not generalities.
- Focus on behaviors, not personalities.
- Collaboratively create improvement plans.
- Deliver feedback promptly while its performance is still fresh.
- Invite Dialogue to encourage employees to respond to feedback.

Did You Know?

Research shows that employees who receive regular, constructive feedback are **twice as likely to be engaged as** those who only receive annual evaluations.

Supervisor's Tip

Monitoring is not about "catching mistakes." It is about creating a feedback loop that drives improvement and builds trust.

Quick Checklist: Monitoring Performance

- Do I monitor performance consistently across all team members?

- Have I clearly explained how performance is measured?

- Am I providing feedback regularly, not just once a year?

- Do I balance between recognizing strengths and growth areas?

Reflection Box

- How do I currently monitor performance?

- Do employees view my monitoring as fair and supportive?

- What one change can I make to improve performance evaluation this quarter?

Section 3: Addressing Underperformance and Promoting Accountability

Even with clear expectations and consistent monitoring, some employees will fall short of standards. In government, underperformance can be particularly damaging, eroding citizen trust and straining limited resources. Supervisors must address issues promptly, fairly, and constructively.

Common Causes of Underperformance

1. **Lack of Clarity** – The employee does not fully understand what is expected of them.

2. **Skill Gaps** – The employee lacks training or resources.

3. **Low Motivation** – The employee feels disengaged or

unrecognized.

4. **Personal Challenges** – Stress, health issues, or external circumstances can impact performance.

5. **Resistance to Change** – The employee struggles to adapt to new systems or processes.

Supervisor's Role in Addressing Underperformance

- **Diagnose the Cause** – Before taking action, supervisors must determine why performance is slipping.

- **Provide Support** – Offer training, mentoring, or resources if the issue is skill-related.

- **Set Clear Improvement Plans** – Document expectations, timelines, and consequences.

- **Hold Accountability Conversations** – Address issues directly, but with respect and empathy.

- **Escalate When Necessary** – If improvement does not occur, follow formal disciplinary procedures.

Supervisor's Tip

Treat underperformance as a problem to solve, not a person to punish. Accountability means helping employees succeed, not setting them up for failure.

Promoting a Culture of Accountability

Accountability should not only apply when problems arise. Supervisors can build a proactive culture where responsibility is part of daily work:

- Set collective goals and track progress openly.

- Celebrate accountability by recognizing employees who take ownership of their work.

- Model accountability by admitting mistakes and correcting them.

- Ensure consequences are applied consistently, reinforcing fairness.

Did You Know?

Research indicates that organizations with strong accountability cultures experience **60% higher employee performance** than those with weak accountability systems.

Quick Checklist: Addressing Underperformance

- Have I identified the root cause of the issue?
- Am I providing resources or training to support improvement?
- Have I set clear, documented expectations and timelines?
- Am I applying accountability consistently and fairly?

Reflection Box

- Which team member needs an accountability chat?
- Can I frame it in a way that supports growth rather than punishment?
- What can I do to strengthen a culture of team accountability?

Case Snapshot: County Health Department

A county health department struggled with delays in processing vaccination records. Citizens complained of long wait times, and public trust began to erode. Investigation revealed that one staff member consistently failed to meet documentation deadlines.

Rather than resorting immediately to discipline, the supervisor met with the employee to understand the cause of the issue. She discovered the staff member lacked proper training in the new electronic system. The supervisor arranged for peer mentoring and set a clear improvement plan with weekly check-ins.

Within two months, the employee's performance improved dramatically. The backlog was cleared, and citizen satisfaction rose. By addressing the issue constructively, the supervisor not only resolved underperformance but also demonstrated fairness and commitment to employee growth.

Practice Exercise

Accountability Action Plan

1. Identify one recurring performance issue on your team.

2. Diagnose the cause: lack of clarity, skill, motivation, personal challenge, or resistance to change.

3. Draft an improvement plan that includes:

    o   Clear performance expectations.

    o   Specific support or training.

    o   A timeline for improvement.

    o   A follow-up plan.

4. Share the plan with the employee to ensure mutual understanding.

5. Track progress and adjust as needed.

Reflection Questions

- Do I address underperformance promptly, or do I avoid difficult conversations?

- Can I strike a balance with accountability, empathy, and fairness?

- What steps can I take to integrate accountability into our daily team culture, rather than relying solely on it as a disciplinary tool?

Summary and Key Takeaways

- Accountability in government ensures fairness, efficiency, and public trust.

- Supervisors must set clear expectations and define measurable performance standards.

- Monitoring and evaluation should be consistent, transparent, and focused on both strengths and areas for improvement.

- Addressing underperformance requires diagnosing causes, providing support, and setting clear improvement plans.

- A culture of accountability develops when supervisors model responsibility and consistently apply standards.

"Accountability is not about blame — it is about ownership. Teams that own their responsibilities earn the trust of the people they serve."

10 BUILDING RESILIENT TEAMS

Introduction

Resilience is the ability of a team to recover quickly from challenges, adapt to change, and continue performing under pressure. In government work, resilience is not a luxury — it is a necessity. Public-sector teams face crises ranging from natural disasters and public health emergencies to budget cuts and political shifts. When these events occur, resilient teams maintain focus, protect morale, and deliver services even under strain.

Supervisors play a pivotal role in fostering resilience. They set the tone during crises, provide stability in uncertain times, and help employees reframe setbacks as opportunities for growth. Without resilience, teams buckle under stress, disengage, or burn out. With resilience, they bounce back stronger, more cohesive, and better prepared for future challenges.

This chapter explores the concept of resilience in the public sector, examines practical strategies for building resilient teams, and discusses approaches to sustaining employee well-being. By developing resilience, supervisors equip their teams not only to survive difficulties but to thrive despite them.

Section 1: Understanding Resilience in the Public Sector Context

Defining Resilience

Resilience is more than endurance. It is not simply "getting through" hard times but adapting in ways that improve capacity for the future. In government, resilience means the ability to maintain services, uphold accountability, and protect public trust while navigating stressors and uncertainty.

Unique Pressures on Public-Sector Teams

- **Constant Scrutiny** – Every decision is subject to scrutiny by citizens, the media, or elected officials.

- **Resource Limitations** – Teams often must deliver more with less.

- **Complex Stakeholders** – Multiple interests, from unions to community groups, create competing pressures.

- **Crisis Frequency** – Public agencies are first responders to emergencies, from storms to pandemics.

Why Resilience Matters

- Resilient teams sustain high performance during prolonged challenges.

- Resilience reduces turnover by enabling employees to manage stress effectively.

- Citizens gain confidence when they see government teams remain calm and effective in the face of pressure.

Supervisor's Tip

Resilience is not about being unshakable — it is about being flexible. Teach your team to bend without breaking.

Quick Checklist: Understanding Resilience

- Do my employees understand resilience as a form of growth, not just survival?

- Have I acknowledged the unique pressures of public-sector teams?

- Can my team articulate how resilience benefits both employees and the broader community?

Reflection Box

- How has my team demonstrated resilience in the past?
- What challenges revealed cracks in our resilience?
- What lessons can we carry forward into future crises?

Section 2: Strategies for Building Team Resilience

Resilience can be cultivated. Supervisors who intentionally embed resilience practices into daily work prepare their teams to handle both predictable challenges and crises.

1. Foster a Culture of Trust and Support

Resilient teams know they can rely on each other. Supervisors should encourage openness, emphasize fairness, and consistently model the expected behavior. When trust is high, teams recover from setbacks more quickly.

2. Encourage Flexibility

Rigid teams struggle under changing circumstances. Supervisors can build adaptability by cross-training employees, rotating roles, and encouraging innovation. For example, training administrative staff in basic field tasks ensures coverage when crises stretch capacity.

3. Strengthen Communication

In times of stress, communication often breaks down. Resilient teams maintain frequent, transparent updates. Supervisors should establish reliable channels, such as team huddles, emergency protocols, and clear decision-making hierarchies, to ensure effective communication and decision-making.

4. Emphasize Purpose

When employees see their work as meaningful, they endure challenges with greater resolve. Reminding teams of public mission - contextualizes setbacks and motivates persistence.

5. Provide Training for Crisis Readiness

Preparedness builds confidence. Simulated drills, tabletop exercises, or scenario planning give employees practice in responding to emergencies. A parks department that runs mock storm cleanups, for instance, will react more effectively when an actual storm hits.

6. Celebrate Recovery and Growth

After a crisis, supervisors should highlight the lessons learned and recognize employee contributions. Celebrating resilience reinforces the team's confidence and ensures institutional knowledge is preserved.

Did You Know?

Research indicates that teams that practice resilience strategies regularly are **40% less likely** to experience burnout during crises.

Supervisor's Tip

Build resilience in calm times. A crisis is the worst moment to start teaching adaptability.

Quick Checklist: Building Resilience

- Have I created a culture of trust and fairness?
- Are employees flexible enough to provide cross-coverage?
- Do we maintain transparent communication during stress?
- Have I connected our resilience to the agency's mission?
- Do we debrief after challenges to celebrate growth?
- Do employees have access to sufficient training opportunities?

Reflection Box

- What resilience strategies are already working in my team?
- What gaps would be exposed in a crisis?
- How can I support my team in building resilience this quarter?
- How do I model resilience in my own leadership?

Section 3: Supporting Employee Well-Being and Mental Health

Resilience is inseparable from well-being. Teams cannot sustain high performance if employees are mentally, emotionally, or physically exhausted. In the public sector, where workloads are heavy and public pressure is constant, supervisors must intentionally support employee well-being.

Recognizing Signs of Strain

Supervisors should stay alert for indicators of burnout or declining mental health:

- Increased absenteeism

- Declining productivity or errors

- Withdrawal from team interaction

- Irritability or conflict with colleagues

- Expressions of cynicism or hopelessness

Early recognition allows supervisors to intervene with support before issues escalate.

Strategies for Supporting Well-Being

1. **Promote Work-Life Balance** – Encourage use of leave, respect boundaries after hours, and provide flexibility when possible.

2. **Encourage Breaks and Downtime** – Even short pauses reduce stress and increase focus. Supervisors should model this behavior by taking reasonable breaks themselves.

3. **Provide Access to Resources** – Ensure employees are aware of Employee Assistance Programs (EAPs), counseling services, or wellness programs.

4. **Normalize Conversations About Stress** – Discussing well-being reduces stigma and helps employees feel more supported.

5. **Recognize Limits** – Supervisors must acknowledge when workloads are unsustainable and advocate for additional resources or adjustments to ensure a sustainable workload.

Supervisor's Tip

Taking care of your team's well-being is not a distraction from the mission — it is essential to sustaining it.

Quick Checklist: Supporting Well-Being

- Do I monitor for signs of burnout?
- Have I encouraged employees to use wellness resources?
- Am I modeling a healthy work-life balance?
- Do I normalize open conversations about stress?
- Have I adjusted workloads when demands became unrealistic?

Reflection Box

- How does my team currently manage stress?
- What well-being practices can I introduce or reinforce this month?
- How can I model resilience and balance for my employees?

Case Snapshot: Emergency Management Team

A city emergency management team faced relentless pressure during a year of hurricanes and flooding. Employees worked long hours, sacrificing personal time and rest. Burnout sets in, leading to mistakes and a decline in morale.

The supervisor recognized the problem and implemented several measures:

- Instituted rotating shifts to ensure everyone had time off.
- Partnered with the city's wellness office to provide on-site counseling.
- Began weekly debrief sessions, allowing staff to share experiences and support one another.
- Publicly recognized the sacrifices employees were making, reinforcing their value.

These actions restored morale and improved performance. The team not only managed the immediate crisis but also emerged stronger, with practices in place to sustain resilience for future emergencies.

Practice Exercise

Resilience and Well-Being Action Plan

1. Conduct a brief, anonymous survey to gauge employees' perceptions of their workload, stress levels, and support.

2. Identify one resilience-building strategy (e.g., cross-training, team huddles) and one well-being initiative (e.g., flexible scheduling, peer check-ins) to implement this month.

3. Create a resilience debrief after your next challenge: What worked, what did not, and what should we do differently?

4. Share lessons learned and celebrate successes as a team.

Reflection Questions

- How do I currently support my team's resilience and well-being?

- Should I address stress proactively, or only after it has become a burnout?

- What resilience practices can I institutionalize to sustain them in the long term?

- How do I model balance, adaptability, and calm for my team?

Summary and Key Takeaways

- Resilience is the ability to adapt, recover, and grow in the face of challenges.

- Public-sector teams face unique pressures — scrutiny, limited resources, complex stakeholders, and crisis response — making resilience essential.

- Supervisors build resilience by fostering trust, encouraging flexibility, strengthening communication, emphasizing purpose, and preparing for crises.

- Supporting well-being and mental health ensures resilience is sustainable.

- Real-world examples demonstrate that resilience strategies not only enhance performance but also bolster morale and decrease turnover.

"Resilience is not just surviving the storm — it is learning to dance in the rain, together as a team."

11 Enhancing Team Innovation and Problem-Solving

Introduction

Government teams are often perceived as rigid and bureaucratic, but the reality is that innovation and problem-solving are just as critical in the public sector as in private organizations. Citizens expect timely and practical solutions to complex issues — from traffic congestion to digital access and emergency response. Supervisors play a crucial role in fostering innovation by creating an environment where employees feel empowered to think creatively and collaboratively solve problems.

Innovation in government does not always mean radical transformation. Sometimes, the most impactful improvements come from small changes — a simplified form, a new communication channel, or a more efficient process. What sets high-performing teams apart is their willingness to question assumptions, explore alternatives, and test new ideas while striking a balance between accountability and fairness.

This chapter explores how supervisors can cultivate creative thinking, utilize structured problem-solving frameworks, and guide their teams in developing innovative solutions. By integrating innovation into daily practices, supervisors enable their teams to deliver better services, build community trust, and adapt to future challenges.

Section 1: Encouraging Creative Thinking and Idea Generation

Creativity enables teams to view problems from multiple perspectives and devise solutions that extend beyond the obvious. In government, where resources are limited and demands are high, creative solutions often stretch budgets further and improve citizen satisfaction.

Barriers to Creativity

- **Risk Aversion** – Employees fear mistakes will draw criticism from citizens or leadership.

- **Bureaucracy** – Layers of approval discourage experimentation.
- **Fixed Mindsets** – Long-tenured staff may resist change, relying on "the way we have always done it."
- **Limited Resources** – Teams may feel they lack the time or funding to try new approaches.

Strategies to Encourage Creativity

1. **Model Curiosity** – Supervisors should ask "What if?" questions and encourage exploration.

2. **Create Safe Spaces for Ideas** – Establish meetings where all ideas are welcomed before being critiqued and evaluated.

3. **Encourage Diverse Perspectives** – Diversity of thought leads to stronger solutions. Invite input from across roles, generations, and departments.

4. **Allow Small Experiments** – Pilot programs or trial runs reduce risk and build confidence.

5. **Reward Initiative** – Recognize employees who propose improvements, even if not all ideas succeed.

Example

A municipal records office faced long wait times. Instead of hiring more staff, the supervisor encouraged brainstorming. An employee suggested staggering appointment slots to reduce bottlenecks. This low-cost idea reduced wait times significantly and boosted citizen satisfaction.

Supervisor's Tip

Creativity does not have to cost money. Sometimes the simplest ideas — often suggested by frontline staff — make the most significant difference.

Quick Checklist: Encouraging Creativity

- Do I welcome all ideas before evaluating them?
- Am I rewarding initiative and experimentation?

- Have I created a safe environment where employees feel comfortable taking risks?
- Do I seek input from a diverse range of voices?

Reflection Box

- When was the last time my team generated a new idea?
- What barriers might prevent creativity in our workplace?
- How can I create more opportunities for brainstorming and experimentation?

Section 2: Using Problem-Solving Frameworks in Team Settings

Creativity sparks ideas, but structure is necessary to transform those ideas into practical solutions. Problem-solving frameworks help teams analyze issues, evaluate options, and implement effective responses.

1. The PDCA Cycle (Plan-Do-Check-Act)

- **Plan** – Identify the problem and design a potential solution.
- **Do** – Implement the solution on a small scale.
- **Check** – Evaluate results against expectations.
- **Act** – Standardize the successful solution or adjust based on feedback.

This cycle works well in government, allowing for cautious, step-by-step innovation while maintaining accountability and transparency.

1. **Root Cause Analysis ("The 5 Whys")**

Teams often address symptoms rather than root problems. By repeatedly asking "Why?" (usually five times), teams uncover the underlying cause. For example, if a city frequently misses trash collection deadlines:

- Why? Trucks break down.
- Why? Maintenance is inconsistent.

- Why? Funding for preventive maintenance is insufficient. The actual issue is not employee performance, but rather the allocation of resources.

3. Strengths, Weaknesses, Opportunities, Threats (SWOT)

This structured framework helps teams assess internal and external factors that influence a challenge. A parks department can use SWOT Analysis to weigh resources, risks, and community needs when planning a recreation program.

4. Collaborative Decision-Making Tools

Supervisors can use methods like dot-voting, consensus workshops, or ranking exercises to prioritize solutions fairly and transparently. These methods ensure all voices are heard and reduce perceptions of favoritism.

Example

A county IT department used the PDCA cycle to address recurring system outages. Following small-scale testing of the new monitoring software, the team evaluated its performance, refined the system, and ultimately rolled out the change across the agency. Outages dropped significantly, and employees felt a sense of ownership over the solution because they were part of the process.

Did You Know?

Teams that use structured problem-solving methods are **30% more likely** to implement successful innovations than those relying solely on ad hoc discussions.

Supervisor's Tip

Frameworks provide guardrails for creativity. They give teams the freedom to innovate while ensuring accountability and fairness in decision-making.

Quick Checklist: Problem-Solving Frameworks

- Do we use structured methods for analyzing challenges?
- Are we addressing root causes, not just symptoms?

- Do employees understand how decisions are made and prioritized?

- Have we tested solutions on a small scale before rolling them out on a broader scale?

Reflection Box

- Which problem-solving framework could I introduce to my team this month?

- How can I strike a balance between creativity and structure in decision-making?

- What is one recurring issue we can tackle using a structured process?

12 SUSTAINING HIGH PERFORMANCE OVER TIME

Introduction

Achieving high performance is a significant accomplishment, but sustaining it over months and years is the actual test of leadership. In government agencies, where political priorities shift, budgets fluctuate, and crises emerge unexpectedly, it is easy for teams to lose momentum after initial success. A team may rally during a new initiative or crisis, but then drift back into old habits once the urgency fades.

Sustaining performance requires supervisors to strike a balance between stability and continuous growth. Employees must be reminded of their mission, recognized for their contributions, and encouraged to improve without burning out. Supervisors must also guard against complacency, ensuring that high performance does not become a one-time peak but an enduring standard.

This chapter examines strategies for sustaining momentum, continually improving processes, and establishing a legacy of excellence in public service. Supervisors who master these practices ensure that their teams not only achieve high performance but also sustain it over time, benefiting the communities they serve.

Section 1: Maintaining Momentum and Preventing Complacency

When teams reach a level of high performance, complacency often follows. Employees may feel the mission has been accomplished, or they may settle into routines that gradually erode performance. In government, where public trust is fragile, even slight declines in service quality can have significant consequences.

Signs of Complacency

- Decline in innovation or initiative.

- Employees are showing less urgency or engagement.

- Increased reliance on "the way we have always done it."

- Resistance to new projects or challenges.

Strategies to Maintain Momentum

1. **Celebrate Success — But Keep Setting New Goals**
   Recognition of achievements is important, but supervisors should pair celebrations with new challenges to foster ongoing growth and development. For example, after a city planning department meets its permit processing targets, the supervisor might set a new goal to improve citizen communication about timelines.

2. **Regularly Revisit the Mission**

   Remind employees why their work matters. Connecting routine tasks to public impact keeps the team focused and motivated.

3. **Encourage Continuous Learning**
   Provide opportunities for training, mentoring, or cross-department collaboration. New challenges prevent stagnation and broaden skill sets.

4. **Introduce Healthy Competition**
   Friendly comparisons can spark motivation without undermining collaboration, such as recognizing the team that responds to service requests the fastest.

5. **Refresh Processes and Practices**
   Even successful processes should be reviewed periodically to ensure ongoing effectiveness. What worked well last year may no longer be efficient in today's environment.

Supervisor's Tip

Momentum fades when teams lose sight of purpose. Anchor performance in mission, not just metrics.

Quick Checklist: Maintaining Momentum

- Have I celebrated achievements while setting new goals?

- Do I connect daily work to the agency's larger mission?

- Am I encouraging ongoing learning and growth?

- Do I regularly review and refresh my processes?

Reflection Box

- Where is my team showing signs of complacency?

- What new challenges or goals can I introduce to re-energize performance?

- How often do I revisit and reinforce the mission?

Section 2: Continuously Improving Processes and Practices

High performance is not a destination but a journey. Continuous improvement ensures that teams adapt to changing needs and remain effective over time. In government, with limited resources and high scrutiny, minor, consistent improvements can deliver the desired results.

Principles of Continuous Improvement

- **Incremental Change** – Focus on minor, manageable adjustments rather than massive overhauls.

- **Employee Involvement** – Involve staff in identifying inefficiencies and suggesting improvements.

- **Data-Driven Decisions** – Utilize metrics, citizen feedback, and audits to inform and guide improvements.

- **Learning from Mistakes** – Encourage a culture where mistakes are examined for lessons rather than punished.

Frameworks for Improvement

1. **Lean and Six Sigma Principles** – Streamline processes by eliminating waste and focusing on quality. For example, a DMV

might streamline license processing steps without compromising security.

2. **Kaizen Mindset** – Encourage employees to suggest minor daily improvements that add up over time.

3. **Benchmarking** – Compare performance with other agencies or jurisdictions to identify gaps and opportunities.

Example

A county public health department noticed that appointment no-show rates for clinics were high. Instead of accepting this as inevitable, the supervisor led a continuous improvement effort. Staff analyzed patterns, discovered that reminder calls reduced no-shows, and implemented an automated text reminder system. Within six months, attendance improved by 25%.

Did You Know?

Studies show that organizations committed to continuous improvement are **30% more efficient** over time than those that rely on one-time initiatives.

Supervisor's Tip

Improvement does not require perfection. Encourage your team to test, learn, and adjust regularly.

Quick Checklist: Continuous Improvement

- Do I review team processes regularly for inefficiencies?
- Am I encouraging employees to suggest minor improvements?
- Do I use data and feedback to guide changes?
- Am I benchmarking performance against peers or standards?

Reflection Box

- What process in my team is outdated or inefficient?
- Can I involve employees in identifying areas for improvement?

- What small change can we implement this month that will have a lasting impact?

Section 3: Building a Legacy of Excellence in Public Service

High performance sustained over time creates something larger than individual achievements: a legacy of excellence. For public-sector teams, this legacy builds trust with citizens, sets standards for future employees, and ensures continuity of service across administrations.

Why Legacy Matters

Government work is often generational — employees serve for decades, and agencies exist across centuries. When supervisors foster enduring excellence, they leave behind systems, cultures, and values that outlast their tenure. This continuity is vital in ensuring fairness, transparency, and consistent quality of service.

How Supervisors Build a Legacy

1. **Document and Share Knowledge**
   Capture lessons learned, best practices, and process improvements in manuals or digital repositories to ensure they are readily available for future reference and review. Prevent institutional knowledge from being lost when employees retire.

2. **Develop Future Leaders**
   Mentor employees, delegate leadership opportunities, and encourage professional development. A legacy of excellence depends on preparing the next generation of supervisors.

3. **Institutionalize Positive Practices**
   Make improvements part of policy and culture rather than one-time initiatives. For example, if a team implements citizen feedback surveys, embed them into standard procedures.

4. **Celebrate Service and Values**
   Reinforce that excellence in government is not just about efficiency but about fairness, respect, and commitment to the public good. Celebrate employees who embody these values.

5. **Model Accountability and Integrity**
   Legacy is shaped as much by example as by systems. Supervisors who lead with fairness, honesty, and humility inspire employees to carry those values forward.

Supervisor's Tip

Legacy is not about your name being remembered — it is about the standards and systems you leave behind for others to build upon.

Quick Checklist: Building a Legacy

- Am I documenting lessons learned and sharing them widely?

- Have I identified and mentored future leaders on my team?

- Are our improvements integrated into daily practice, or are they one-time fixes?

- Do I celebrate employees who embody public service values?

- Am I modeling the integrity and accountability I want to see continued?

Reflection Box

- What practices on my team should outlast my tenure?

- Who am I mentoring to carry forward our culture of excellence?

- What legacy of values and performance do I want my team to be known for?

Case Snapshot: City Parks and Recreation Department

A city's parks and recreation department faced years of declining resources and public dissatisfaction. Citizens complained of unkempt parks and canceled programs. A new supervisor inherited the department at its lowest point.

Rather than focusing only on immediate fixes, she set out to build a long-term legacy. She implemented a system of community volunteer days, trained staff to take ownership of specific parks, and documented maintenance standards in a publicly available manual. She also mentored several younger employees, preparing them to step into leadership roles.

Ten years later, even after the supervisor retired, the systems and culture she built remained. Volunteer days had become a community tradition, staff maintained high standards, and new leaders carried forward her values. Citizens saw not just improvement but continuity — evidence of a legacy of excellence in public service.

Practice Exercise

Team Sustainability Planning

1. Ask your team to identify one current practice that should continue for the next five years.

2. Discuss how to document and institutionalize that practice so it survives staff turnover.

3. Identify one future leader in your team and create a development plan for them.

4. As a group, draft a short "legacy statement" describing the standards and values you want your team to be known for.

5. Revisit the statement quarterly to ensure actions align with the legacy you are building.

Reflection Questions

- What systems or practices will remain in place after I leave this role?

- How am I preparing my team to sustain high performance in the long term?

- Am I effectively mentoring the next generation of leaders?

- What do I want my team's legacy to be in the eyes of citizens?

Summary and Key Takeaways

- Sustaining high performance requires vigilance against complacency and ongoing commitment to improvement.

- Supervisors must celebrate success while setting new goals, regularly revisit the mission, and foster continuous learning.

- Continuous improvement frameworks enable teams to adapt processes and maintain efficiency over time.

- Building a legacy of excellence means documenting lessons, mentoring future leaders, institutionalizing best practices, and modeling public service values.

- Sustained high performance ensures not just short-term wins but lasting trust and excellence in government service.

"High performance is not an event — it is a habit. Build it daily, and you create a legacy that endures long after you are gone."

APPENDICES

Appendix A

Glossary of Key Terms

Accountability – The obligation of supervisors and employees to take responsibility for their actions, decisions, and performance, ensuring fairness and transparency in government service.

Adjourning – The final stage of team development, where a group disbands after completing its task or project. In government work, supervisors must ensure knowledge is documented before the team dissolves.

Bureaucracy – The system of rules, procedures, and administrative structures that govern public organizations, designed to promote fairness and consistency but often criticized for slowing decision-making.

Change Management – A structured approach to guiding teams through organizational transitions, policy reforms, or new systems while minimizing resistance and maintaining morale.

Collaboration – The process of individuals or departments working together to achieve shared goals, often across organizational boundaries.

Conflict Resolution – The process of addressing disagreements or disputes among team members to restore collaboration and trust.

Continuous Improvement – An approach to problem-solving that emphasizes ongoing, incremental enhancements in processes, efficiency, and service delivery.

Delegation – The act of assigning responsibility and authority to employees for specific tasks, while holding them accountable for outcomes.

Diversity – The presence of differences in backgrounds, experiences, perspectives, and demographics within a team. In government, this extends to generational, cultural, and professional diversity.

Emotional Intelligence (EI) – The ability to recognize, understand, and manage one's own emotions while also empathizing with and responding effectively to others.

Empowerment – Granting employees the authority, autonomy, and resources to make decisions and take ownership of their work.

Feedback – Constructive input provided by supervisors to guide employee performance, including both recognition of strengths and identification of areas for improvement.

Forming, Storming, Norming, Performing – The stages of Bruce Tuckman's team development model, commonly applied in public-sector leadership.

Innovation – The application of new ideas, processes, or technologies to improve performance, solve problems, and enhance service delivery.

Innovation Pilots – Small-scale trials of new ideas or processes before broader implementation, reducing risk and building confidence.

Leadership Development – Programs, experiences, and self-reflection that help supervisors grow into stronger leaders capable of guiding public-sector teams effectively.

Mentorship – A professional relationship in which a more experienced employee guides and develops a less experienced colleague.

Organizational Culture – The shared values, behaviors, and norms that shape how employees interact and make decisions within an agency.

Performance Standards – Clearly defined expectations for quality, timeliness, and consistency of work, used by supervisors to measure accountability.

Public Trust – The confidence that citizens place in government agencies and employees to act reasonably, transparently, and in the community's best interest.

Recognition – Formal or informal acknowledgment of an employee's effort, contribution, or success, often critical in sustaining motivation.

Resilience – The ability of a team to recover, adapt, and thrive in the face of challenges, crises, or change.

Self-Reflection – A practice by which supervisors examine their actions, decisions, and impact on others to improve leadership effectiveness.

Stakeholders – Individuals, groups, or organizations with an interest in the outcomes of government services, such as citizens, elected officials, unions, and advocacy groups.

Transparency – The practice of openly sharing information, decisions, and processes so employees and citizens understand how government operates.

Trust – Confidence in the integrity, fairness, and reliability of supervisors and team members, serving as the foundation for collaboration and accountability.

Well-Being – The overall mental, emotional, and physical health of employees, directly influencing resilience and long-term performance.

Appendix B

Recommended Reading and References

Scholarly Works

- Fernandez, S., & Moldogaziev, T. (2020). Employee Empowerment and Performance in the Public Sector. Public Administration Review.

- Hvidman, U., & Andersen, S. C. (2019). Impact of Performance Management in Public Organizations. Journal of Public Administration Research and Theory.

- Riccucci, N. (2019). Public Administration: Traditions of Inquiry and Philosophies of Knowledge. Georgetown University Press.

- Wright, B. E., Hassan, S., & Park, J. (2021). Transformational Leadership in Public Organizations: Effects on Follower Attitudes and Performance. Review of Public Personnel Administration.

Practical and Professional Resources

- Blanchard, K., & Johnson, S. (2019). The New One Minute Manager. HarperCollins.

- Buckingham, M., & Goodall, A. (2019). Nine Lies About Work: A Freethinking Leader's Guide to the Real World. Harvard Business Review Press.

- Covey, S. R. (2020). The 7 Habits of Highly Effective People (30th Anniversary Edition). Simon & Schuster.

- Grant, A. (2021). Think Again: The Power of Knowing What You Do not Know. Viking.

- Heath, C., & Heath, D. (2020). Upstream: The Quest to Solve Problems Before They Happen. Avid Reader Press.

Appendix C

Supervisor Self-Assessment Tool
Rate each item on a scale of 1–5 (1 = Rarely, 5 = Always).

Team Foundations

- I have communicated a clear vision for my team.
- My employees understand their roles and responsibilities.
- I regularly connect our work to the agency's mission.

Communication & Trust

- I listen actively and encourage employees to share their thoughts and ideas.
- I communicate openly, honestly, and consistently.
- I model fairness and integrity in my decisions.

Performance & Accountability

- I set clear expectations and measurable standards for my team.
- I monitor performance consistently and provide timely feedback.
- I address underperformance directly and constructively.

Resilience & Innovation

- I support employee well-being and adaptability in times of stress.
- I encourage creative problem-solving and innovative thinking.
- I celebrate resilience and lessons learned after challenges.

Leadership Growth

- I invest in my own leadership development.
- I mentor and develop future leaders within my team.
- I reflect regularly on my strengths and areas for improvement.

Scoring:

13–30: Developing – Focus on building consistency in your supervisory practices.

31–50: Emerging Leader – You demonstrate many effective habits but may need deeper reflection and refinement.

51–65: Effective Leader – You are practicing strong leadership and building accountability, but continue to pursue continuous growth.

66–75: High-Performing Supervisor – You model excellence in leadership and are well-positioned to mentor others.

ABOUT THE AUTHOR

Dr. Patrick C. Patrong is a seasoned leader, author, and consultant with more than 30 years of experience in public service and organizational development. He is the President of Patrong Enterprises, Inc., where he designs and delivers innovative leadership development programs for government agencies, universities, and community organizations.

Dr. Patrong holds a Doctorate in Strategic Leadership and is a certified Lean Six Sigma Black Belt. His expertise spans leadership development, performance evaluation, and employee engagement, with a particular focus on helping supervisors and managers navigate the challenges of accountability, trust, and collaboration in the public sector.

As a speaker and facilitator, he is recognized for his engaging "magic with a message" approach, which seamlessly combines practical strategies with memorable illustrations. His programs, such as the Supervisory Learning Experience and the PAAL™ System (Posture, Attire, Attitude, Language), have inspired leaders across state and local governments to transform the way they manage people and performance.

Beyond his professional work, Dr. Patrong is a dedicated mentor and lifelong learner who believes that leadership is not a position but a practice. His passion is captured in his guiding philosophy: *"Transforming Organizations – One Employee at a Time."*

www.ingramcontent.com/pod-product-compliance
Lightning Source LLC
Chambersburg PA
CBHW072019060426
42446CB00044B/2948